Managing the crowd

rethinking records management
for the Web 2.0 world

Managing the crowd
rethinking records management
for the Web 2.0 world

Steve Bailey

facet publishing

© Steve Bailey 2008

Published by Facet Publishing
7 Ridgmount Street, London WC1E 7AE
www.facetpublishing.co.uk

Facet Publishing is wholly owned by CILIP: the Chartered
Institute of Library and Information Professionals.

Steve Bailey has asserted his right under the Copyright,
Designs and Patents Act 1988 to be identified as the author of
this work.

First published 2008

British Library Cataloguing in Publication Data
A catalogue record for this book is available from the British
Library.

ISBN 978-1-85604-641-1

Typeset from author's disk in 11/16pt Bergamo and Unitus by
Facet Publishing.
Printed and made in Great Britain by MPG Books Ltd,
Bodmin, Cornwall.

Dedication

For Claire and 'the bump'

And for my parents, for all their love
and support over the years

Contents

Foreword

GIVEN THE NATURE of this book, I think it wise to spend a little time at the outset explaining what this book is *not*. This may seem a rather odd way to commence, perhaps even a touch negative, but I believe it to be important in terms of establishing the context for this work and maybe for managing readers' expectations.

This book is not a handbook, a manual or even a guide to Web 2.0 and records management. As a consequence, those who are seeking any form of indispensible 'How to' book which provides clear step-by-step instruction on how to manage Web 2.0 information within their organization may well be disappointed; though, in my defence, I would argue that anyone claiming to have produced such a work at this point in time is almost certainly guilty of exaggeration, with its readers destined to be left sorely disappointed. This, then, is the truth that lies at the heart of this book and which is largely responsible for the path it has taken: not only do we not currently know the answers, we are only just beginning to understand the questions.

Nor, I'm afraid, can much of this book be described as 'optimistic'. In many respects, much of what follows is an explanation of the unprecedented size and scale of the challenge that faces us, of how records management currently falls short in terms of a response, and of the likely consequences of our unpreparedness. This may not always be comfortable to read (nor for me to write) but is, I believe, perhaps the single most important job this book has to do, for without first convincing the reader of the very real and immediate challenges ahead, and the severe limitations of the professional tools we have at our disposal, we lack the incentive to change. After all, if the status quo is rosy, why bother to think (or indeed read) beyond it? The danger is, of course, that repeated proclamations of the imminent coming of the apocalypse can understandably breed an air of fatalistic resignation that helps nobody. Thankfully for us, the very force that is responsible for hurling this maelstrom towards us also brings with it the exact same tools we need to tame it and to manage it – but that is for a later chapter . . .

Neither should the reader expect this book to represent a new approach to *all* aspects of records management, which will sweep away all before it and render every facet of current practice obsolete. It is true that much of what I say does raise serious questions regarding the fitness for purpose of our existing methodology, but only in relation to the management of information created and held in Web 2.0 systems and services. This is an important point to grasp from the outset; when I draw attention to the weaknesses and failings of the way we currently do things this is not a sweeping statement intended to imply that it is now redundant across the board. As we shall see, it is the rise of Web 2.0, and particularly its Office 2.0 offshoot, that represents an overwhelming challenge to the status quo. It is only where these ripples are being felt that this book applies; the logical corollary of this is that there therefore remains a vast swathe of the records management profession where the contents of this book do not apply – at least not yet. In some cases this may be particular processes or the records created by them, in other instances it might be complete organizations or perhaps (at a push) even entire sectors which currently seem unaffected. Where this is true I have no qualms about saying that much of this book will not apply – at least (and here it is again) not yet.

So, here we have a book that provides few answers and seemingly little hope, and that only applies to a small subset of the records management profession and the information it seeks to control. After such a sales pitch you may well ask why anyone should bother reading it at all; a question to which I would offer the following points in its defence.

Firstly, it views our profession from a completely different perspective: regardless of how many records management books you may have read, I can guarantee that this is *not* just more of the same. An integral part of this new perspective is that it does not assume that records management is self-evidently and unquestionably important in its own right. To my mind, that is a badge that it has to earn on merit and not just inherit without question. We should never forget (and hopefully this book never does) that records management is only the means to an end and is not, nor ever should be considered, the end in itself. With this in mind this book hopefully serves a useful, and rather novel, function by actually daring to ask what the new and emerging 'ends' are that it must support, and how appropriate or otherwise are the means to achieve them that we currently employ.

But challenging the status quo and daring to be different can only be justified if circumstances truly require it, and, unfortunately for us, they do. It is difficult to overstate the gulf that has grown in recent years between the acts of information/records creation and management. Technology has profoundly shifted the balance of power away from the organization and towards the individual, a trend recognized by *Time* magazine when it made 'You' its person of the year for 2006 with a magazine cover claiming 'You control the information age. Welcome to your world'. The rise of Web 2.0 in particular represents the fulcrum of this change. It is a technology that strips away many of the fundamental building blocks on which records management has traditionally been based and its influence is rapidly extending beyond the walls of the organization to pervade virtually every sphere of our cultural, social and economic life.

There is no doubt that the speed at which these changes are being felt currently varies enormously depending on the nature of the organization in which you work; but whether you operate within a risk-hungry, fast, agile development company or within a staid, traditional branch of the civil service it *is* heading your way – it is simply a question of whether it takes months or years before making its presence felt. To date, professional engagement with Web 2.0 seems to have been limited to training events looking at how records managers and archivists can take advantage of these technologies within their own workplace (while conveniently seeming to overlook the fact that it falls squarely within our professional remit to *manage* them). Often allied to this are anguished discussions between records managers as to whether a blog or a wiki really should be described as records (the implication and hope being that if they don't, we don't have to worry). I fully accept that to records managers this has traditionally been seen as a crucial distinction and one which has indeed determined what is within our scope ('records'), and what lies outside it ('information'). As explained in later chapters, this is a distinction which I believe is fast losing its relevance: thus my deliberate use of the terms 'information' and 'content' throughout this book where you may have expected the word 'records' to appear. Where I have used the term 'record' its use is deliberate and hopefully the rationale for doing so is either obvious or explained fully.

And so, finally, to what this book actually *is*. It is an attempt to convince the records management community that a change, the like of which few of us will have seen in our professional careers, is coming. It is an exposé of how and why records management as currently practised will not be fit for the purpose of meeting this challenge, and a warning of the risks both to our profession, and our organizations, that this represents. But it is also more than just a tale of woe and offers examples of how the core values and objectives of records management are still hugely relevant and necessary in this new world – provided we are willing to fundamentally rethink the way in which we strive to achieve them. Chapter 11 presents a series of 10 principles that I believe must be adhered to when we embark on this process of rethinking records management in order to make sure that it meets the specific problems posed by the rise of Web 2.0 while also standing as good a chance as possible of meeting future, as yet unknown, challenges.

Lastly, it suggests some specific examples of how Records Management 2.0 could actually be implemented: a radical new theoretical model that removes the existing dependency of records *management* on the records *manager*, and instead looks to harness the wisdom of the crowd to help manage the crowd. I make no apologies for the speculative nature of these proposals; they are intended as a starting point, the classic 'Aunt Sally' to promote discussion and debate, and should not be simply dismissed just because they do not conform to our pre-conceptions of how records management should be practised.

The world is changing fast and we are in danger of getting left further and further behind. Hopefully, by reading this book, you will be left in no doubt as to the scale of the challenge which confronts us, but will also be left feeling sufficiently encouraged and empowered to help ensure that the records management profession is fully able to meet these challenges, and to perform the role required of it.

Preface

IMAGINE AN ORGANIZATION where users are free to describe the content they create as they see fit. Where they help decide the retention and disposal of every record that they create or use, based on how useful and valuable *they* deem it to be. Where, based on a combination of their thoughts and actions, they are responsible for determining who can use the information they create and who cannot.

To many records managers this probably sounds like a recipe for chaos, an anarchic organization which is out of control and where the user is king – the very antithesis of what records management should strive to achieve. Indeed, many would say that this represents a vision of exactly the kind of future that the records manager is fighting an increasingly desperate rear-guard action to prevent.

But what if, rather than railing against it, we were actively to embrace it? What if just for once the records management profession were not to ignore the march of technology, or to try to fight against it, but to harness it, and to turn it to our advantage, in pursuit of the same fundamental goals and objectives that have driven records management for half a century? What if we were to use the wisdom of the crowd to manage the crowd?

A dozen flaws implicit in this premise probably spring to mind, followed by a hundred scenarios in which it couldn't or wouldn't work – all of which may well prove true. If we had a better alternative these reservations might well be enough to kill such unorthodox views at birth, but the stark fact we must face up to is that we don't. The orthodox approach to managing records is rapidly reaching the limits of its effectiveness. Within a few short years the changes to our organizations, our society and our culture, driven by the new technical paradigm into which we are now moving, threaten to make the way we currently manage our records obsolete.

Anyone doubting the ability of technology to fundamentally change records management should think back to the very origins of the profession itself. For at its core, records management, as we know it both in theory and practice, stemmed largely from the need to find ways of coping with the sudden increase in paper following the introduction of new copying technologies and the eventual invention of the photocopier. In truth, what we as records managers do, and how we do it, has changed little in the decades since. Indeed, the signs are there that many records management programmes are already struggling to cope with the management requirements of current records, as witnessed, for example, by the rash of UK government personal data scandals in late 2007 and early 2008.

We are, therefore, currently presented with a paradox: that the need for the underlying principles and objectives of records management has never been greater; and yet at the same time it has never been more apparent that records management as traditionally practised is not, or will shortly no longer be, fit for purpose.

But we have a choice. We can choose to accept the status quo, or we can challenge it. We can keep trying to squeeze the last drops of life from a methodology designed for another age, or we can invent a new one. Some may say that to do so would mean abandoning our professional principles; I would disagree. What this book attempts to do is to demonstrate that those principles are more needed today than ever, but in order to realize them we have to be willing to think again, and even to start from scratch. You may disagree with some of the solutions proposed in this book – perhaps even all of them – but if at the end of it you have been stirred into thinking of just one other approach that might be worth consideration it will have served its purpose.

I am indebted to the following people for their support and encouragement during the writing of this book: Dr Gill Ferrell, David Ryan, Helen Carley, Janet Jones and, above all, my wonderful wife, Claire, to whom I owe so much.

Steve Bailey

PART 1

The nature of the changing world

CHAPTER 1

The big picture: Web 2.0 and current trends in IT

Questions addressed in this chapter

- What defines Web 2.0?
- How does it differ from Web 1.0 and what do they have in common?
- What are some of the other trends in IT and information creation that are influencing, or influenced by, the rise of Web 2.0?

What is Web 2.0?

You don't need to be an IT professional to have noticed the rapid rise of a new breed of web applications and services over the past couple of years. Names such as YouTube, Facebook and Wikipedia have seemingly appeared from nowhere to become part of the cultural mainstream almost overnight. And these represent just the tip of a very big iceberg, one which is commonly known as Web 2.0.

It must be acknowledged at the outset that this is not a term or even a concept accepted by all and is indeed disputed by such luminaries as the man credited with the invention of the world wide web itself.[1] But equally, there exists a growing body of evidence and band of supporters who perceive a significant enough change, both in the technology and in the way in which it is being utilized, to support the assertion that what we are now witnessing does indeed represent a new, second iteration of the world wide web.

That said, the scepticism of Tim Berners-Lee and others should at least serve to remind us that any definition of Web 2.0 is bound to be imperfect, open to challenge and likely to change over time – so too the type and range of services and applications that may be said to fall under its umbrella.

It is possible to identify at least seven distinct types of Web 2.0 application (van Harmelen, 2007) and in many respects it is through such a list that we can most usefully define what we currently mean by Web 2.0.

According to van Harmelen these seven types of Web 2.0 software include:

1   Blogs
2   Wikis
3   Social bookmarking
4   Media-sharing services
5   Social networking systems
6   Collaborative editing tools
7   Syndication and notification technologies.

But while the above list tells us something of the type of web service that can be described as 'Web 2.0', it does little to clarify what it is that actually differentiates them from their Web 1.0 predecessors. To do this we need to focus our attention away from the underlying technology and towards the respective role of the user in both the Web 1.0 and Web 2.0 worlds.

Since its invention in the early 1990s the user experience of the world wide web has been a largely passive one. Within most organizations web content has been produced by a relatively small and limited clique comprising those with the technical ability to produce web pages and the authority within organizations to publish 'approved' output. In this respect, though the delivery mechanism was very different, the basic model underpinning Web 1.0 closely mirrored that of traditional publishing, with content being provided by a limited number of sources and the consumer having little choice but to either read, or ignore, the information being provided. There was comparatively little potential for active or innovative reuse of the material and what feedback mechanisms existed were limited, stilted and 'artificial'.

Web 2.0 has turned this model on its head; the floodgates are well and truly open and we are all potential content creators now. Sites such as YouTube, Flickr and Wikipedia not only encourage the individual user to contribute content, they are totally reliant upon it. Without the tens or hundreds of thousands of individuals choosing to upload their favourite video clips or images, there would be no content. But it doesn't end there. For every user who contributes content there might be another dozen who comment on it, rank it, link it to related material, take it and embed it into their blog, or reuse it for another purpose. Web 2.0 is a world without walls where content is king and the potential for its use and reuse limited only by the imagination of the individual user.

Rather more surprisingly, these services are nearly always provided free of charge – at least for the basic level service. This is something we are rapidly taking for granted but which is a radical departure from the accepted rules of business. This has undoubtedly been a decisive factor in the explosion in growth that such services have witnessed in the past couple of years. It has helped form the massive user base that is an essential prerequisite of all Web 2.0 applications and services, reliant as they are not only on the presence but on the active participation of massive numbers of individual users, sometimes referred to in this context as 'the crowd'.

It is for this reason that the records management community cannot afford to turn a blind eye to the implications of Web 2.0. The web is no longer a passive publishing vehicle, something which we can take advantage of for our own purposes but largely dismiss as an area of professional concern. Just as we have long acknowledged and agonized over the fact that our users conduct business transactions via e-mail and therefore create records in e-mail (despite its unsuitability as a technology for the purpose),[2] so the same will be true with Web 2.0. If the defining characteristic of Web 2.0 is the creation, sharing and repurposing of information by individual users we have to acknowledge that this surely places this technology and its use firmly and squarely in the back yard of the records management profession.

Similarities and differences compared to Web 1.0

But if it is this notion of the web as a platform, rather than just a publishing vehicle, that most differentiates it from what has gone before, this does not mean that Web 2.0 has nothing in common with its predecessor. Many of its characteristics have actually been an integral part of the world wide web since its inception over a decade ago and are likely to continue to be equally pertinent in the Web 2.0 world. Upon first glance some of these qualities appear so obvious and self-evident as to be unworthy of comment but, as we shall see, though often previously taken for granted, their significance to the management of information should not be underestimated – a significance which will, if anything, increase with the rise of Web 2.0.

Firstly, the vast majority of the content and services available online via the web are generated and provided by external agents over which your organization has no control. When the web was simply a source of reference material it could be argued that this was little different from the pre-online era, where staff may have relied just as heavily on printed journals, magazines, text books and broadcast media – all of which too originated from external sources. But now that these services are also providing the *applications* being used by staff, and *storing* the content they create, the implications of this may be far more significant.

One of the consequences of the remote nature of the web is that it requires little by way of client technology to function. A PC or laptop, a modem, a browser and some anti-virus software are the minimum required. This is a very different model to the application-heavy burden placed on the user's PC by the standard office software suite, where operating systems and software applications have to be physically installed and located on the local hardware. This is, of course, a feature closely related to the external nature of the web and, as we shall see, it is responsible for further weakening the ties of dependency that currently bind users to the internal IT infrastructure of their organization.

A final characteristic shared by both the Web 1.0 and Web 2.0 worlds is their transience. Some researchers claim the average life expectancy of a web page to be less than two months, while the bursting of the dot-com bubble in the late 1990s taught many investors the hard way that little in the online world possesses the kind of stability and longevity that breeds long-term trust. Even in the short period of time that Web 2.0 has been making the news it has been possible to see the fortunes of individual services wax and wane. A year ago MySpace was seen as the great online phenomenon; now that crown is (at the time of writing at least) being worn by Facebook. But in this fickle and fast-moving world how long will it be before this too is eclipsed by some new and currently unknown social software wunderkind? We have already identified that Web 2.0 services rely on the presence and participation of the crowd to function. Whereas in the Web 1.0 world a drop off in visitor numbers might have caused a slow steady decline in advertising revenues that might eventually have threatened the long-term viability of traditional websites, the desertion of the crowd is likely to have a much more sudden, profound and irrevocable impact on the prospects of Web 2.0 services.

This will naturally be a key cause of concern for the records manager. For as a profession we are used to taking the long view, not only looking at the value of information for today, but at its potential relevance in the future. We are rightly careful to ensure that we take whatever measures are needed to ensure the survival and accessibility of records in the future, be that by the creation of back-up copies, by format migration, or by ensuring the suitability of the physical storage environment. Such measures help maximize the chance of survival of the records we believe we will need into the future, and are largely possible because the items in question are within our possession and held within our own hands (be they physical or virtual). What impact will the reliance of our users – and potentially our organizations – on external service providers have on this ability, and what additional risks may it create in an uncertain technical and commercial world?

IT trends: blurring the boundaries

'Thanks. Interesting.
But shouldn't you put these up on YouTube, where they can be commented on, embedded and linked to, like everyone else does?'

This was one immediate e-mail response received by an organization after publicly announcing that it had just made two short research and development videos freely available on its website; though brief it encapsulates an interesting new by-product of the Web 2.0 world.

Sites such as YouTube and Flickr have now attained such market dominance that it is rapidly becoming inconceivable that any organization should bother to reinvent the wheel and develop its own facility for storing and sharing its own content. It is clear from the above quote that the author of the e-mail considers YouTube the natural home for online video clips. The chances are that he (or she) uses it extensively for both domestic and work purposes. He is likely to be an active account user who is familiar with the service offered and, more importantly, knows that he can make use of other Web 2.0 applications to repurpose the content and make maximum use of it in a variety of different contexts.

Evidence is emerging that this is not a phenomenon restricted to media-sharing services such as YouTube or Flickr. A recent report commissioned into the use of Web 2.0 within the UK Higher Education sector uncovered examples of academics who are eschewing the formal systems provided by their institutions, such as the Virtual Learning Environment, and are choosing instead to use Facebook as their preferred means of keeping in contact with their students (Anderson, 2007).

Such examples not only help demonstrate that Web 2.0 applications are already beginning to have a very real impact on some sectors, but also how they are beginning to blur the boundaries between domestic and business use of IT. It is achieving this by becoming users' first and preferred service in both spheres of their life. Of course this has been true for many years in terms of people's common use of Microsoft Office applications or Google both at home or in the office, but that was very different. In these examples the applications may have represented common tools, but were tools largely being used for very different and distinct purposes. By using them to write a budget report at work and a letter to their child's school at home the traditional boundaries between office and domestic life remained largely intact. Plus, of course, though it may have been the same product being used in both examples, the chances are that it will have been two physically different instances of that product in use.

The crucial difference with Web 2.0 services such as YouTube, Flickr, Facebook and the like is that they are content storage repositories as well. They no longer just represent the tools, but also the filing cabinet: filing cabinets that now contain side by side the combined outputs from both our domestic and work life. What is more, because of the core concepts of data reuse and manipulation underpinning Web 2.0, users are now likely to make use of content created in one part of their life as part of their role in the other without a second thought (for example using a photograph taken during a weekend family outing and stored on Flickr to illustrate a point in a presentation they create the next day for a team meeting at work).

IT trends: the exponential age

'In a world with infinite storage, bandwidth, and CPU power, here's what we could do with consumer products . . . Store 100% of User Data. With infinite storage, we can house all user files, including: e-mails, web history, pictures, bookmarks, etc and make it accessible from anywhere.'[3] Volume is now everything. The above quote from a leaked internal Google presentation demonstrates how, for Google, the seemingly boundless growth in storage capacity has the potential to revolutionize the world.

Most of us will be familiar with Moore's Law (the 'law' first articulated by Dr Graham Moore in 1965, revised in 1975, which states that the number of transistors on a chip will double every 24 months),[4] which has proved a remarkably accurate prediction of the growth in storage capacity over the past 30 years. The even more powerful and unbeatable laws of physics must surely dictate that one day Moore's Law must fail – that we shall reach a point at which it is physically impossible to cram ever more technology into even less space, or that we shall run out of the energy required to power the vast server farms required by companies such as Google. But there are few signs that we will reach either point any time soon. In fact, every time the chip industry seems to run up against a seemingly insurmountable obstacle to keeping pace with Moore's prediction, a new technical breakthrough occurs to keep it on track: for example with the recent replacement of the silicon dioxide traditionally used to make the gate dielectrics within transistors with the metal hafnium – a change described by Graham Moore himself as 'the biggest change in transistor technology since the late 1960s'.[5]

Evidence of the impact of continual storage growth is all around us and shaping our daily lives. Take the popular Yahoo! e-mail service for example. When it launched in 1997 it offered its users 4Mb storage for their e-mail accounts; by 2004 that figure had soared to 100Mb. In May 2007 the company took the next logical step and now offers all of its users unlimited e-mail storage. The vision of the future described by John Kremer, Vice-President of Yahoo! Mail, when announcing this development has clear parallels with Google's view of where we are heading: 'We hope we're setting a precedent for the future. Someday, can you imagine a hard drive that you can never fill? Never having to empty your photo card on your camera to get space back? Enough storage to fit the world's music, and then some, on your iPod? Sounds like a future without limits.'[6]

The participation of the crowd, mass media storage and the ability to continually repurpose content – all inherent characteristics of Web 2.0 – would not be possible without access to the levels of storage capacity we now take for granted.

These technical developments are also having an impact far beyond the world of IT and records management, and represent one of the most powerful forces shaping popular culture and user behaviour in today's world. Ten years ago a fortnight family holiday meant taking a couple of 24-exposure camera films and doing your best to spread them out over the two weeks. Now we can take that amount of pictures or more every hour and, should we wish to, choose to keep every image.

Then there is the web itself, providing the user with free and instant access to several billion pages of information. People may occasionally complain that they can't find what they are looking for, but seldom call for it to be reduced in size. Thanks to Google and the like we now have a new generation emerging who would far rather *search for* than *manage* information, and who value quantity over quality. Indeed this trend is even beginning to influence the information management profession itself, as the following quote from *Information World Review* makes clear: 'Information is inherently disorganised and not uniformly stored, and it is better to provide good search than to provide good organisation of the information.'[7]

If we were to accept this train of thought, where would this leave the records management profession, a profession based on an underlying assumption of centralized control? Indeed, given that most of the central tenets of records management practice were defined in the pre-electronic age when the volume of records being created was a fraction of that created today, it begs the question: is records management scalable enough?

It is not uncommon to hear information professionals rather smugly dismiss Google and its inaccuracy, pointing to the fact that every search brings back several million web pages in its results, and comparing this unfavourably to their tightly defined, metadata-controlled search engine which only returns a handful of relevant hits. But this is to miss the point entirely. The user couldn't care less about the six million other results that Google has returned, because almost without fail the information they are looking for appears at, or very near, the top of the list. The number of times the user needs to refer to the second or subsequent pages of results is, in my experience, rare: and this is through simple basic searching. What is more, it has required no effort on behalf of the content creator, or the end user. No need to follow metadata schemas, consider classification schemes, or add additional keywords.

All the while Google focused on being a web search engine the genie was still just about in its bottle. Users may have been happy to rely on Google to retrieve and rank four million hits when it came to the internet, but were still – within reason – willing to think of their internal documents in a different light and to continue to file things according to their organizational file plan and add metadata where necessary.

A host of new desktop search engines such as Copernic[8] and Google desktop[9] are rapidly changing this and bringing the same logic of cheap storage and easy retrieval to the contents of our PCs and laptops. Users are now able to see just how easy it is to retrieve their files, regardless of the folder they have put them in, or what they have been called, and with absolutely no decision making or manual input required on their behalf.

If more proof where ever needed that volume and retrieval technologies are the undisputed drivers behind IT, take a look at the companies listed on the Nasdaq-100 Technology Sector Index.[10] The majority of the IT behemoths listed either relate to storage (Intel, SanDisk, Oracle, Sun, etc.) or, to a lesser extent (thanks to Google's dominance one suspects), search. Far less prominent are those companies dealing with the classification, management and disposal of information. Put simply: storage sells; disposal doesn't!

As the American blogger Karl Fisch succinctly puts it: 'We are living in exponential times.'[11] His excellent presentation *Did you know?* contains a barrage of fascinating statistics to ram home this point, one of the most telling of all being 'The amount of new technical information is doubling every two years . . . it is predicted to double every 72 hours by 2010'[12] – a sobering statistic which reminds us that what we are seeing today, though profound in itself, is but the tip of the iceberg that lies ahead.

References

Anderson, P. (2007) *What is Web 2.0? Ideas, technologies and implications for education*, www.jisc.ac.uk/media/documents/ techwatch/tsw0701 bword.doc [accessed 3 March 2007].

van Harmelen, M. (2007) *Briefing Paper on Web 2.0 Technologies for Content Sharing: Web 2.0, an introduction*, http://franklin-consulting.co.uk/LinkedDocuments/Introduction%20to%20Web%202.doc [accessed 5 October 2007].

Notes

1 A transcript of a podcast interview of Tim Berners-Lee, inventor of the web, www-128.ibm.com/developerworks/podcast/dwi/cm-int082206.txt [accessed 5 October 2007].

2 Due largely to the range of formal and informal purposes that e-mail is commonly used for, the nature of most e-mail applications (which makes the acts of creation and replication far easier than management), and the common misconception that this has led to that e-mail is an ephemeral and untraceable medium.

3 http://blog.outer-court.com/archive/2006-07-11-n52.html [accessed 16 July 2007].

4 http://en.wikipedia.org/wiki/Moore%27s_law [accessed 2 March 2008].

5 http://news.bbc.co.uk/1/hi/technology/7002267.stm [accessed 19 September 2007].

6 http://ymailuk.com/blog1/2007/03/28/yahoo-mail-goes-to-infinity-and-beyond/ [accessed 20 September 2007].

7 Beyond Search, *Information World Review*, **229** (November 2006), 2–21.

8 www.copernic.com/ [accessed 3 March 2008].

9 http://desktop.google.com/ [accessed 3 March 2008].

10 www.nasdaq.com/services/indexes/ViewIndexes/Nasdaq_tech.
aspx?symbol=NDXT [accessed 2 February 2008].

11 http://thefischbowl.blogspot.com/ [accessed 2 February 2008].

12 http://thefischbowl.blogspot.com/2006/08/did-you-know.html
[accessed 2 February 2008].

CHAPTER 2

The reality check: surely change is endemic in IT?

Questions addressed in this chapter

- Is Web 2.0 simply the latest stage in a continuum of IT change?
- How different is the office of today from the workplace of 1997 and what does this tell us about the nature of the change likely to accompany Web 2.0?
- Is it possible to identify major 'paradigms' within the history of IT development, and if so, how has records management responded to them?

Change as the only constant in IT

Everybody knows that the only constant thing in IT is change. If the last 20 or 30 years have taught us anything it is surely that the forward march of technology is relentless and unstoppable. At a superficial level one only has to view with our 21st century eyes how Hollywood was portraying cutting-edge technology in the 1980s, in films such as *War Games* for example, to see how laughably outdated and obsolete it all looks. Scenes set in offices filled with green screens displaying jerky vector graphics, printers spewing out ream after continuous ream of hole-punched printer paper and actors struggling to lift house-brick heavy mobile phones to their ears.

Even within our own lives and experiences we can see obvious echoes of this change. Contrast the size and speed of your first laptop with the sleek, slim-line model you currently use; the complex line commands of DOS compared with the familiarity and ease of use of Windows; the speed of an 8MB domestic broadband service as opposed to the slow torture of a dial-up connection.

Change is the oxygen that the IT industry breathes. Without it there is no improvement and, more importantly, no incentive for the user to upgrade. Satisfaction with the status quo is not good for sales. No sooner have you taken the plunge and bought their latest model than you see advertisements in the press proudly announcing the launch of their next model, which sweeps away all before it. Of course, within the IT industry the motivation for change is also largely driven by ever increasing capacity, and the constant pushing of technical and engineering boundaries by some of the world's largest research and development budgets. More efficient hardware enables the development of more complex applications, which in turn empower the user to undertake evermore advanced activities. As a result, today's apparent IT nirvana is tomorrow's arcane museum piece.

Surely when viewed in this context the rise of Web 2.0 described in the previous chapter is simply the latest in a long line of small, iterative steps which may appear new and radical today, but which will rapidly be taken for granted before equally quickly being superseded. Hasn't records management been here before – seen the arrival of an apparent new technical era and managed to come to terms with it, meet its challenges and carry on regardless?

When viewed in this light many sceptical readers, particularly records managers, may be thinking that the previous chapter overstates the case: that change has always been the defining factor of IT and as such that Web 2.0 is simply the latest manifestation of this change. Yes, the growth of a new collaborative, user-created, content-rich version of the world wide web might be a fairly radical step forward – but it is surely only that: the next logical step in what will be a very long, and more than likely never-ending, journey. We didn't feel the need to start questioning the fundamentals on which records management theory is based with the rise of the PC in the 1970s and 80s, nor with Web 1.0 in the 90s, so why get so exercised now? More especially as the fundamental tenets on which records management is founded are supposed to be timeless, like the lighthouse that continues to fulfil a vital function with metronomic regularity, regardless of the ever changing nature of the seas that crash around it. It's a comforting idea, but is it really sustainable?

The familiarity of the office of 1997

Let's start by looking more closely at the assumption of constant and consistent levels of IT change, and how the rise of Web 2.0 fits into this picture. The year 2007 marks the tenth anniversary of my first job in records management. Looking back at the pharmaceutical company I then worked for, the way we operated and the tools we used, I see the past less like a foreign country and more like the familiar interior of my own home.

Firstly, back in 1997 all staff had access to a desktop PC. Admittedly with their 1GB hard drives and Pentium120 processors they are dwarfed by the power of today's machines, but nonetheless they were all networked, with full read/write access to the contents of shared file servers which were accessible to all relevant teams, functions or departments to store and share their documentary outputs. The vast majority of those outputs were created by the core suite of Microsoft Office applications that are still so very familiar to us today. As with today, these applications had a physical presence on the user's PC, were maintained by our central IT staff and upgraded en masse when new service packs, anti-virus software or versions were required – so far, so familiar.

We used e-mail as our regular, perhaps even main, form of internal communication: the volume of messages received certainly eclipsing by some margin the number of memos and other hardcopy correspondence received courtesy of the internal mail service. E-mail was also regularly used to transfer documents and other attachments, particularly when working with staff in other areas of the business that did not have access to the file server. Amazing as it may seem, by 1998 the organization had already recognized the limitations of these approaches and was piloting its first document management system. We were even designing a photographic archive system available via our company intranet which not only acted as a catalogue for our physical photographic library but even as the repository for the growing number of digital photos beginning to be taken by the corporate services department.

Mention of the intranet serves to remind us that a decade ago the internet and world wide web were already well established technologies, fully integrated into our daily work as a source of reference material and a vehicle for the organization to advertise its work and celebrate its achievements. Meanwhile, structured information was being managed in relational databases and even raw data, the outputs of the pharmaceutical R&D process, were being stored and managed in their native digital format via a 'Central Electronic Archive'.

So, while at a superficial level everything seems to have changed in the past decade – the power of the hardware at our disposal, the complexity of the application we use, the volume of information at our fingertips – in reality the fundamentals of how we use technology and the way in which it is integrated and managed within our organizations have essentially stayed the same. Despite a decade of innovation it is still largely a case of 'as you were' for information creation and management, and we are still operating within the same basic *IT paradigm* as we were a decade ago – but for how much longer?

The first IT paradigm

It is certainly a matter for conjecture and debate, but I would argue that in the past 30 years we have only witnessed two true paradigm shifts in IT, with the rise of Web 2.0 promising to be the third, and perhaps most radical yet. The first was the invention and widespread adoption of the PC during the early 1980s where 'killer applications' such as VisiCalc and WordPerfect made possible the automation of office life and cemented the client-server architecture as the default model for a generation of organizations and their staff. It is possible to trace a consistent and steady development path from these origins through the picture of office life I described from 1997 to the underlying IT infrastructure on which most organizations still depend today.

It is interesting to reflect on how the records management profession responded to the dawning of the PC era and the client-server age. I must confess that my own age (or lack of it!) prevents me from being able to draw upon first hand experience, but, from my professional training and research, it would seem that our basic approach was to seek to apply the same techniques and methodologies formulated 30 years earlier to cope with a paper-based world. Initially, by insisting on the printing out of electronic memos, documents and e-mails and treating them as hardcopy records and, latterly, when that approach became untenable, by trying to manage electronic records as simply physical records without form. Thus, electronic records were organized within classification schemes designed to replicate paper registry systems and the processes of retention, appraisal and disposal continued as before, regardless of format. When the volume of electronic records was still comparatively small it can be argued that such traditional approaches were largely able to keep pace but, as we shall explore in more detail in later chapters, as the volume and diversity of electronic information *increased*, so the relevance and effectiveness of records management as we know it to cope with this change *decreased* by equal measure. These pressures – already evident to those honest enough to look them in the eye in the pre-Web 2.0 world – are, as we shall see later, likely to prove insurmountable for records management as we move into the Web 2.0 era.

The second IT paradigm

But before moving from the first to the third paradigm we must, of course, consider the second: that is the introduction and phenomenal growth of the world wide web (which for the purposes of this book I am describing as Web 1.0) during the 1990s. Perhaps surprisingly – given the way in which it has transformed business, commerce, society and culture – there is actually comparatively little to say about the impact of Web 1.0 on the way organizations create and use internal information, at least from the records manager's perspective.

It is hard to summarize the impact that the world wide web has had on the developed world since the early 1990s in a way that does it sufficient justice. Thankfully, such has been the all-pervasive nature of its reach into all aspects of our life that I can be confident that every single reader of this book will have experienced it for themselves. Maybe through using the world wide web as a reference source; conducting e-business transactions to buy books, DVDs or book holidays; checking the process of a planning application; or renewing your car tax via an e-government portal. The web is now a fully integrated aspect of our culture and our lives, fuelled by the ever increasing speed, and decreasing costs, of domestic broadband connections, and the rise of mobile wireless devices. The web no longer sits alone in splendid isolation. Every newspaper, every television channel and radio station have their own 'value added' online interactive services, all helping to break down traditional cultural and media silos.

Most organizations treated Web 1.0 as a publishing vehicle and part of the 'shop window' used to display information about their organization to the wider world. It's difficult to generalize about the range of content likely to be featured on the average organization's website during the 1990s and first years of the 21st century, but press announcements, product information, corporate brochures, investor information and contact details often featured large. Websites were usually designed and maintained by the organization's corporate affairs or marketing departments, reflecting the external-facing nature of most of the site's content and rarely, it seemed, with the active participation of the records manager.

Of course, that is not to say that a corporate website never included the kind of internal business record which fell well and truly under the remit of the records management programme. Annual reports, statements of account and human resources policies were often featured on websites. But even where they did, the link between the website and records management programme was often non-existent, at least from any interactive, interdependent perspective. The version of the Annual Report hosted on the website was usually deemed to represent a copy, rarely, if ever, the original version. This allowed the records manager to continue to manage their master copy (either physical or electronic) as they had always done, and prevented the need to influence the management of the version hosted on the website.

My choice of a self-contained, structured document such as the Annual Report was a deliberate one, reflecting the fact that what involvement records managers did have with their website was almost always restricted to such content. Rarely did records management programmes extend their remit to actively dictating the lifecycle of the countless individual pages of HTML that formed the main part of most websites.

Of course, none of this prevented records managers from being enthusiastic and voracious *consumers* of the web: our repositories had websites, our services web pages. Maybe we even offered online access to finding aids, digital copies of records to requestors, or a web front end to our databases. But as I say, these were all ways of consuming the internet, and seldom led to an active contribution to the management of the information that was created and shared by it.

The question this raises is whether either of the following approaches, both of which were favoured by records managers in coping with the first and second IT paradigms, is inappropriate as we begin to enter what I believe will represent the third IT paradigm: the Web 2.0 era. Can records managers again act as passive passengers as we did with Web 1.0, or if we are to play a more active management role should we simply seek to apply, with some minor tweaking, the traditional techniques and methodologies that have served records management for half a century, as we did in response to the rise of the PC? To answer these questions we must examine in more detail the nature of Web 2.0, its implications for the way in which our organizations create and manage information, and the role records management as traditionally conceived may be able to play in this new world.

CHAPTER 3

Web 2.0 and Office 2.0: enter the third paradigm

Questions addressed in this chapter

- Who *owns* a blog: the author, or their organization?
- Can we manage a wiki as a corporate resource?
- Why are collaborative editing tools different from traditional Office applications?
- Why are users happy to 'tag' for themselves in social software applications, but resist adding 'metadata' within corporate systems?

After a brief sojourn in the recent IT and information-creating past, it is time to return to a consideration of the present and a projection into the future. So far, our overview of the essential nature of the new Web 2.0 era has dwelt largely upon what are currently its two most obvious expressions: social networking systems and media-sharing services. Some of the effects these technologies may have on the way information is created and manipulated have already been touched upon, particularly the volume of data created, the potential for repurposing and reuse and the erosion of the traditional barriers between work and home. These in themselves should all be enough to excite the interest of the records manager, but as mentioned back in Chapter 1, these represent only two of the seven identified types of Web 2.0 service or application; so what of the other five?

At this point it is perhaps worth reminding ourselves of the full list of Web 2.0 service types, which includes:

1   Blogs
2   Wikis
3   Social bookmarking
4   Media-sharing services
5   Social networking systems
6   Collaborative editing tools
7   Syndication and notification technologies[1]

In terms of their potential impact on the way in which our organizations create information it is appropriate to leave consideration of social bookmarking and syndication and notification technologies to one side for the moment, as both are more concerned with the selection and management of information rather than its creation. Though, as we shall see, it is these tools which offer significant potential for the records manager when seeking to extend their influence to this domain, and their role as such will form an important element of later chapters.

Blogs

The web log, or blog, is another of the most visible expressions of Web 2.0. The Technorati Blog aggregation service suggests there are currently somewhere in excess of 100 million blogs in existence.[2] The blog is effectively a single web page in which the author writes a series of posts, each in chronological order, with the newest post displayed at the top of the page. Readers are encouraged to submit comments on what they have read with the original blogger often choosing to respond directly to comments posted. Readers may come across blogs by a variety of routes: they may see a reference to it in another medium (perhaps a magazine article or on another website); it may have been retrieved by a search engine during a general search for information of relevance to a particular subject; or they may have found reference to it on another blog. In this regard the world of the blog can appear an insular one with bloggers frequently either linking to, or commenting on, postings to another blog. This has quickly created a vast network of interconnected blogs producing a web–like structure closely akin to the world wide web itself.

Blogs exhibit many of the essential characteristics already identified in relation to other Web 2.0 technologies. With over 100 million active blogs it is clear that this is not a publishing vehicle restricted to the few: here is a means by which any member of 'the crowd' can be heard. Nor do blogs represent one-way traffic, encouraging as they do the active participation of their readership. Blogs also exhibit the same qualities of flexibility and reusability that is evident in all other flavours of Web 2.0. It is easy to embed a blog within a broader website, or to embed images stored on Flickr and the like into your blog. Blogs, as with media sharing services, social networking systems and all other aspects of Web 2.0, can either function in isolation or form an integrated element of a greater whole. This is the Web 2.0 application as a building block which can serve a useful function on its own, but which becomes even more powerful when added to other blocks to create an infinite range of bespoke and complex structures.

A quick browse through Technorati gives a flavour of the almost unimaginable range of topics on which people blog: from the banal and the bizarre to the serious and the sexual, just about all aspects of human nature seem to be represented. But for the purposes of this book and for records managers, the most interesting area is what can perhaps be best described as the professional blog. Take a look at the website of any major IT company and you will see it now includes at least one, and often more, such blogs. These are often maintained by key members of the organization such as board members, chief designers or developers and are used as a kind of running commentary about developments on new projects and initiatives within the organization. There are countless examples of this trend, but prominent examples include: Microsoft Community Blogs,[3] IBM[4] and Google.[5]

The professional blog raises interesting questions for the records manager about its ownership, function and management, in particular relating to the blurring of the division between a user's personal and work life. This point can best be illustrated with reference to my own experience. Since May 2007 I have been posting to a blog I created to explore issues of relevance to the future of records management.[6] This stemmed from my desire to be able to communicate any odd thoughts or observations which I may have about records management to a wider audience and to stimulate debate, but on an occasional, ad hoc basis, rather than through more formal journal papers or articles. As my organization does not currently host or provide access to any internally maintained blogging software I opted to use the popular, free Blogger[7] service offered by Google. Sometimes, the topics I post about are directly related to my official work role, perhaps announcing the launch of a new initiative or commenting on an event which my organization has paid for me to attend. Meanwhile, at other times, blog posts might be stimulated by something I have read in the weekend newspapers, or heard on the radio and have nothing whatsoever to do with my day job. Similarly, I might sometimes write a post towards the end of my working day, but during work hours; whereas on other occasions the urge to write may come during the evenings or at weekends.

The only two common threads which run through this scenario are myself as the author and the future of records management as the subject. Everything else is almost completely intertwined and inseparable and certainly when it comes to writing a post I never stop to think whether I am, or should be, writing it while wearing my 'work hat' or my 'personal hat'. On the one hand, anything I write does, to a greater or lesser degree, reflect on the organization I currently work for and as such represents one of the increasingly diverse ways in which we, as an organization, communicate with our stakeholders. And yet, if I were ever to change job and work for another organization, the chances are that I would continue to maintain the blog from my new vantage point. Leaving to one side for the moment questions regarding the format of the blog as a 'record', it is clear that this new medium and more importantly the way in which it is routinely used, fundamentally challenges our traditional notion of what represents a corporate record.

One obvious path through this fog, and one which will reappear again and again in terms of how we approach the management of Web 2.0 resources, is to bring the technology within the walls of the organization. If my organization were able to provide me with its own internal, officially sanctioned blogging software this would surely help clarify things significantly. After all, anything I wrote on the organization's blog would belong to the organization and equally be their responsibility to manage. This would inevitably manifest itself as a policy I would have to follow in terms of what is, and isn't, suitable material for me to post on, accompanied by sanctions that could be imposed if I fail to comply. This would significantly alter the tone, purpose and usefulness of the blog and would decrease my interest and motivation in maintaining it. Having the freedom to write about a range of subjects that far exceeds the remit of my organization is important to me, as is the ability to comment with candour, to challenge and on occasion to be deliberately provocative. Of course I could create and maintain a second blog in my personal capacity which ticks these boxes, but maintaining two blogs in parallel about the same subject matter and sometimes even addressing the same specific topic, but from two differing perspectives, would seem a shade ridiculous. It would not only be frustrating to me and to any potential readers, but would also introduce false barriers and force me into adopting a split personality which I would soon find unsustainable. I would be the first to acknowledge that one of the advantages of working in the higher education sector is that it provides me with a greater degree of freedom of expression than would be the case if I were employed in many other sectors, such as the civil service, where such choices would not necessarily be open to me at all. But it will be interesting to see what impact the emergence of a new generation of the best and brightest potential staff will have: people who have grown up considering their blogging activity to be a non-negotiable and natural extension of their life, and who cannot conceive of working for an organization that denies it to them.

Wikis

The origin of the word Wiki is said to come from the Hawaiian word for 'quick'. According to Wikipedia, itself perhaps the best known exemplar of the technology, a wiki is described as:

> a medium which can be edited by anyone with access to it, and provides an easy method for linking from one page to another. Wikis are typically collaborative websites, though there are now also single-user offline implementations. Ward Cunningham, developer of the first wiki, WikiWikiWeb, originally described it as "the simplest online database that could possibly work".[8]

Many organizations, project teams and loose associations of individuals have found the wiki to be an invaluable collaborative tool. Being available online via a web browser makes it possible to connect to it from virtually anywhere. It also removes many of the problems often associated with sharing information in any collaborative way between organizations by circumventing issues relating to system compatibility and security firewalls. Text can be drafted, or reviewed, by multiple users in a secure environment and usually with a full audit trail of revisions being retained.

In many respects, wikis are the ultimate expression of the change that has occurred between the Web 1.0 and Web 2.0 eras. A wiki is basically a series of web pages linked together to form a website, but whereas the ability to create, edit and update the contents of the traditional website rested with just one or two people, with the wiki it potentially rests with everyone. Wikipedia is the best known example of the wiki concept and in many respects of the whole Web 2.0 movement. Here is a free online encyclopedia with over 2 million entries in the English language version alone, each one created and donated freely by a member of the public with the knowledge and inclination to do so. It should be a disaster. By rights it should have quickly withered away as people tired of submitting content, or began to resent providing it for free. It should be full of spoof entries, profanities and spam, as the online equivalent of street vandals moved in and claimed the space. It should be wildly unreliable, with every crank, conspiracy-theorist and over-opinionated yet under-informed amateur using it as a sounding board. But amazingly it is none of these things; in fact it works rather well. Of course it is not perfect, far from it. Some critics have a deep fundamental concern at the rise of the cult of the amateur and the threat to genuine expertise and professionalism that it represents (Keen, 2007, 4). On a more practical level, sceptics will point to several well-documented examples of factual inaccuracies within entries which have come to light: some accidental, others malicious. But, by and large, the self-policing of Wikipedia by the hundreds of thousands who use it tends to prevail. Inaccuracies are quickly spotted and corrected and attempts at subversion usually soon snuffed out. Because there is no impermeable barrier separating author from reader, people feel engaged and have a sense of the shared responsibility that stems from shared ownership. Ultimately the *wisdom of the crowd* has won out – at least for now.

Indeed, it is not only the amorphous crowd which appears to be winning. That crowd is, of course, made up of countless individuals and the ease of content creation and dissemination offered by Web 2.0 technology empowers the gifted amateur, the iconoclast and the maverick, all of whose voices can offer so much, but which often go largely unheard thanks to a lack of access to official communication channels. It is intriguing to speculate how Albert Einstein (a mere patent clerk when he first embarked upon his research) would have chosen to communicate his ideas if he were alive today, but one can easily see the advantages that a blog or Wikipedia would have provided in terms of allowing him to quickly, cheaply and easily reach a larger and more influential audience.

Once again, with wikis we must consider the seemingly contra-dictory issues raised by the underlying Web 2.0 concepts of openness and mass participation, and the innate desire of our organizations to own and control information. Wikipedia is, of course, at the extreme end of the spectrum in terms of a concept that could only work in a free and universal manner. As with blogs, many organizations may choose to host and maintain their own wiki systems as in-house systems – thus providing their staff with the functionality they require while retaining clear lines of corporate ownership of the content created within it and the means to manage it. This is probably easier to achieve successfully with wikis than with blogs. The blog usually contains far more of the individual in both its style and its content and is, as a consequence, far more subjective in nature. As we have seen, it is often difficult, if not impossible, to separate what I as an individual records manager may think about an issue from what I as an employee of my organization may think. Use of the wiki on the other hand tends to be more objective. Its purpose is often more defined: to share project documentation; to update the annual report; to prepare a funding bid and so on and it therefore sits more clearly in the corporate space. Even when participation in a wiki-based endeavour extends to users from outside the organization it is usually quite obvious who owns the data created and whose responsibility it is to manage it.

From the records manager's perspective this offers the potential for us to manage wikis along more established, traditional lines. If our organizations own and maintain the wiki software we can influence its design and operation. We can introduce facilities to enable (or enforce) users to add metadata from the corporate schema, or to declare the content as fixed and final records at certain points. We can also introduce applications to enable us to appraise its contents and to manage their retention and disposal along predetermined lines.

Unfortunately, of all the variations of Web 2.0 technology we have identified, this happy state of affairs only really rings true for wikis. As well as the problems of trying to artificially separate blogs into personal and work spaces, we have also seen how leading media-sharing services have attained such market dominance that to build similar repositories *within* the organization's firewalls seems a redundant, retrograde step. Likewise, though the large multi-national company might attempt to implement their own social networking system to help locate and liberate the tacit knowledge that its staff holds, it is difficult to see their popularity eclipsing that of Facebook, Bebo or MySpace anytime soon, given that these provide users with the ability to communicate with the totality of their contacts, irrespective of the particular area of their lives to which they happen to relate.

Collaborative editing tools

Collaborative editing tools represent the last, and in many respects the most significant, incarnation of Web 2.0 from the records manager's perspective.

The list of applications which allow users to create content, to share it, edit it and update it all online, is steadily growing. It is no longer necessary for your PC to have the standard range of 'office applications' installed upon it. Instead, should you choose, there is a range of externally hosted Web 2.0 services such as DocStoc[9] to produce and store text documents, wikiCalc®[10] to create spreadsheets and SlideShare[11] to put together presentations.

But it is not simply that these services now replicate the functionality of Microsoft Office and other such applications, they actually enhance them by combining the power of the tools these packages already provide to the user with the additional advantages brought by the ethos and technology of Web 2.0. Hence the document I create within Googledocs is available to me wherever I might be and via whatever PC I happen to be using, so long as I have access to the internet. It requires no additional software to be installed and leaves no footprint behind on the machine I have been using; it is just there wherever and whenever I need it.

Such tools also enable seamless collaboration between dispersed and disparate users, in much the same way as discussed with the wiki. There is no requirement for all members of a project team to be using the same operating system, to have accounts which enable access via organizational firewalls, or have specific client applications installed on their machines. Once again, all they need is an account with the relevant service and a web browser.

Content can be restricted to just a few individuals or it can be opened up and shared with the world. As with all other flavours of Web 2.0, the content remains *alive*. It can be combined with other sources, repurposed and embedded. For example, the presentation stored on SlideShare which includes images, themselves stored on Picasa, can itself be integrated within a blog. Most systems also enable users to leave feedback on the content, perhaps also to rank and rate it, thus further helping to create a shared sense of ownership and an interest in its well-being. Contrast this vision of limitless creativity and potential with the comparatively dead and lifeless content cemented within the confines of a Word document and it is easy to see which the user is likely to prefer.

Social bookmarking and tagging

This same sense of the content being part of a greater whole is reinforced by the concepts of folksonomies and social bookmarking. Through these technologies, people are free to call the content they create whatever they like and to attach as many labels in the form of 'tags' to it as they wish. Likewise, those who discover the content (by whatever means) are at liberty to either reuse the tags already applied to it (and by doing so helping to reinforce their weight), or to add as many new and different terms as they wish. Once again, this *should* represent a recipe for disaster. Anyone who has ever attempted to implement a system which requires users to manually add metadata knows that unless its addition is made a mandatory condition of use it is rarely, if ever, applied. They also know that even when presented with a carefully designed, quality-assured, pre-populated metadata schema, the accuracy of what is chosen is often questionable. So to leave it completely up to the user whether to add any metadata at all, and if so to call it whatever they want, is surely just madness? And yet, somehow, it seems to work.

Content creators and users in the Web 2.0 world seem to actively *want* to add metadata. Just occasionally, when writing a blog post I will forget to add descriptive tags to it before hitting the 'publish' button, but as soon as I realize I will *always* go back and add them. I know that, thanks to the power of social bookmarking, those labels are the best chance of people finding and reading what I have written. It is not some seemingly pointless bureaucratic exercise but something that is very definitely in my interests and as such I will do it and I will think carefully about how I do it. Likewise, if I stumble across content which I think is interesting and useful I will 'bookmark' it for future reference. And because these same tags and bookmarks are not limited to specific isolated systems I am happy to do so because I immediately see the advantage to me of doing so. Once again, this is not something which is formally controlled or centrally dictated and so seems to break every rule in the book – but with hundreds of thousands of users all doing the same thing via services such as Del.icio.us,[12] Digg[13] and StumbleUpon[14] it works.

The growth of these collaborative editing tools seems to have been largely overlooked by the records management community. Where there has been discussion about Web 2.0 it has largely revolved around its more obvious expressions, such as blogs and wikis, and debates about whether these formats should actually be classed as 'records' (and therefore by extension whether we really need bother about them professionally). However, at the same time and with virtually no discussion or debate, a completely new record-creating and recordkeeping era has emerged and grown at a phenomenal rate. 'Office 2.0' encompasses all the underlying trends, technologies and user-behaviour that we have identified in relation to other forms of Web 2.0, but in a way that is directly and indisputably within the realm of the records manager. If records management is to have relevance and a future which lasts beyond the next five to ten years then we had better start to take note of this development – and fast.

Reference

Keen, A. (2007) *The Cult of the Amateur: how today's internet is killing our culture*, Currency.

Notes

1 http://franklin-consulting.co.uk/LinkedDocuments/Introduction%20to%20Web%202.doc [accessed 2 October 2007].
2 www.technorati.com/ [accessed 2 October 2007].
3 www.microsoft.com/communities/blogs/PortalHome.mspx [accessed 2 October 2007].
4 www.ibm.com/developerworks/db2/community/blogs.html [accessed 2 October 2007].
5 http://googleblog.blogspot.com/ [accessed 2 October 2007].
6 http://rmfuturewatch.blogspot.com [accessed 2 October 2007].
7 www.blogger.com/start [accessed 2 October 2007].
8 http://en.wikipedia.org/wiki/Wiki [accessed 2 October 2007].
9 www.docstoc.com/ [accessed 6 February 2008].
10 www.softwaregarden.com/products/wikicalc/index.html [accessed 6 February 2008].
11 www.slideshare.net/ [accessed 6 February 2008].
12 http://del.icio.us/ [accessed 6 February 2008].
13 www.digg.com/ [accessed 6 February 2008].
14 www.stumbleupon.com/ [accessed 6 February 2008].

CHAPTER 4

Welcome to the world of Office 2.0

Questions addressed in this chapter

- How might Web 2.0 and Office 2.0 be adopted and implemented within an organization?
- What steps might (perhaps inadvertently) lead an organization down this path?
- What might become of the role of the records manager in this world?

The scenario

The fictitious organization described in this chapter is intended as a prediction of how the trends and technologies driving the Web 2.0 movement might change the way in which our workplaces function. So far as it is possible to put a date on when this scenario is set, it could be somewhere within the next five to ten years. However, it should also be remembered that from the technical perspective all that is being described is already available and could be put in place *now*.

Our organization is a medium-sized, private-sector management and business services consultancy company, with around 800 staff. As well as its main central office, it has staff based in various host organizations around the country, and a small team of client managers who spend the vast majority of their time travelling the length and breadth of the country, establishing new contracts and maintaining existing ones.

Outsourcing e-mail

In line with many other companies, our organization chose a few years ago to outsource their e-mail service to Google Mail. It seemed a sensible decision at the time and has proved a very successful and popular one since. Management like it because it has significantly reduced the overheads involved in storing and maintaining an in-house, mission-critical business service. The IT team like it because they had been finding it more and more difficult to provide the 24/7 zero-downtime level of service users were demanding, and now freed from the yoke of maintaining such a service have been able to be much more creatively and usefully employed. And, most importantly of all, the users like it. Of course they now take its reliability for granted (though do still offer up a silent prayer of thanks at 10.30 p.m. on a Sunday evening when, desperate to confirm some information before a meeting the following morning, they find the service is up and running). Users also love the fact that this is a product which has been purpose designed as a web service and provides optimum functionality whenever and wherever they use it, be that in the office, at home or in a hotel.

Perceived limitations of the client-server based document management system

For over a decade, the backbone of the rest of the company's information infrastructure had been their local area network, which provided staff with access to the contents of the organization's servers. These servers housed departmental file stores, databases and line of business applications, such as the finance system. Aside from the usual minor gripes about inconsistent file naming and version control problems, its use was well established as the bedrock of how the company functioned. Staff were strongly encouraged to store all of their work-related documents, spreadsheets and other outputs to the relevant area of their departmental file store, where they could then be subject to the organization's records management policies. Because of the growing volume of records being created, and in line with the fashion of the time, the organization decided to reinforce this existing infrastructure by implementing a document management system. It was believed that this would help enforce the policies and procedures which had hitherto only been carried out in a partial and patchy manner; it was also believed that this move would improve the accuracy and reliability of the information created, and therefore would increase the accountability of the organization as a whole.

Unfortunately, the implementation of the document management system came just at a time when discontent with the restrictions that the current architecture was believed to be placing on users was reaching a peak. Driven partly by commercial pressures and partly by changes in IT, the nature of the organization and pattern of work for many of its staff were changing fast. Staff who had previously spent the vast majority of their working day in the office now found themselves out and 'on the road' on a more regular basis. Trips to client sites, regional meetings and marketing events meant more and more staff found they were spending a significant proportion of their time away from the office, cut off from the corporate knowledge base which existed behind the organization's firewalls. Staff had to try to plan in advance what information they might need and remember to transfer a copy to their laptop before they left, and then remember to return the updated version to the document management system upon their return. This soon proved time-consuming, cumbersome and unpopular. Thankfully, the growing availability of wireless networking soon meant it was possible for staff to access the network drive and the document management system via a Virtual Private Network (VPN), which made it theoretically possible to gain access to information; but the realities of trying to navigate and operate a resource-heavy system, designed for use within a client-server environment, via a slow and fragile wireless connection, often deterred all but the most patient or desperate: it certainly didn't make for seamless and efficient collaboration.

Collaboration was also proving increasingly difficult, not only between staff but with commercial partners and, even more importantly, with clients. IT staff were reluctant to provide 'guest logins' to people from outside the organization, because of the workload involved in processing such requests and the difficulties in identifying exactly which resources they required access to. More often than not, staff resorted to sending draft documents to and fro via e-mail and manually (and with mixed success) managing version control. In particular, those staff based within a client site for the duration of a contract were also struggling. Not all clients were happy for staff to be installing VPN software on their machines, which again left them without access to the corporate knowledge base and feeling cut adrift from the organization.

A successful wiki pilot

Both management and technical staff were becoming increasingly aware of, and concerned about, the limitations their current client-server architecture seemed to be placing on the flexibility and efficiency of the organization. After some research and internal debate, it was decided that a wiki would greatly increase their ability to collaborate, both internally and with selected external contacts. The pros and cons of either hosting their own internal wiki or simply buying a licence to an external service were debated and ultimately it was decided to bring this 'in house'. Though outsourcing the e-mail service had been a success, there were still some reservations on the part of management with regard to the idea of putting all their eggs in one basket – particularly if that basket belonged to someone else. Management was also aware of some sensitivity within the IT team regarding the long-term implications of outsourcing yet another corporate system and what it might mean for their future job security.

The wiki quickly established itself and demonstrated its collaborative credentials. Staff loved the ability to be able to access corporate information wherever and whenever they had access to a web browser. External contacts also appreciated the ability to access the most recent information regarding their project and to add their own contributions in a quick and convenient manner. The wiki was deliberately allowed to grow organically, to enable it to fill gaps wherever a need was perceived. Not unexpectedly, these gaps most often appeared when multiple staff were all working on the same area, such as the preparation of bids, project management and strategic planning activities.

Online applications: the next logical step

Although the wiki was a boon when it came to enabling the quick cut and thrust of collaboration, it was clearly no replacement for the document management system. Its benefits came from allowing staff to share and express ideas and draft text within the wiki editor to be displayed as 'web' pages – not the creating, updating and storing of a final, formatted document or record. So, although the wiki was considered a success, it was clear that significant further obstacles still remained to providing an information management infrastructure that fully met their organizational and user needs.

It was at that point that the staff who had helped the organization to transfer to their externally hosted e-mail service began to take a serious look at the suite of other online applications that the service also provided. It was quickly discovered that word processing documents, financial spreadsheet and presentation slides could also all be housed, maintained and accessed online by the same provider. Given the success of the e-mail project and the only partial solution provided by the wiki, management was persuaded to take a closer look. The advantages seemed obvious. Here was a free service which could provide all their staff with the means to collaborate, in real time, regardless of their physical location or the computer they were working from. Furthermore, this capability could be extended to external partners and clients quickly and easily and as and when the need arose, without having to provide access through firewalls, or install client software. The content hosted by the service was secure, backed up and managed by the same state-of-the-art technical infrastructure that had already proved so reliable and trouble-free for their e-mail. Also, as with their e-mail, there was no limit placed on the volume of information being uploaded or stored and, furthermore, content would be easy to find, thanks to the integration of search-engine technology. And, best of all, the cost of the corporate licence for access to such services was considerably less than the cost of trying to replicate anything similar in-house.

Not surprisingly, senior management was soon sold on the idea. To most it seemed an obvious move to make, which would not only increase the company's flexibility and capability, but would do so while saving significant infrastructure costs on an ongoing basis. Naturally, there were some who felt uneasy about handing over what essentially represented their entire intellectual assets to an external organization. However, this unease was soon dispelled when it was pointed out that the company had been entrusting the hosting of the website and its content to a third party for many years, and its e-mail for several years, without a problem. This move just represented the next logical step in the journey to creating a truly streamlined and cost-effective organization, able to meet its full potential.

Of course a few dissenting voices remained, but then they always do. Those who had invested heavily in trying to make the best of the document management system were not happy to see the fruits of their labours being left to wither on the vine. The records manager, in particular, continued to bang the drum for this corporate resource and to issue warnings about uncontrolled information creation, inefficient retrieval and the dangers inherent in a failure to actively manage retention and disposal. Largely to appease these few but vocal critics, the document management system was allowed to continue. In theory it was supposed to be operating in parallel, but in reality it quickly became a legacy system. The volume of new information being captured by it dwindled to a trickle and users soon began to transfer any existing documents held within it, which related to ongoing live projects, to the new online service.

In a bid to secure a long-term role for the document management system the records manager fought to rebrand it as the 'corporate archive': a quality-assured, managed repository for storing and providing access to the final versions of approved business records. Thus, even if project documentation was being created and actively used elsewhere, at least the finished record, once approved and signed-off, would ultimately reside within the corporate system. It wasn't ideal, but it was better than nothing. It also worked much better in theory than in reality. It soon proved impossible to establish any form of seamless transfer process from the online hosted service back to the document management system and users resented the laborious process it therefore entailed to manually upload records to the document management system. The concept of manually adding metadata, of having to navigate an unfamiliar structure and decide where the record should physically reside within a virtual system, all seemed laborious, anachronistic and largely pointless. And once there, the final record was then divorced from the other information relating to the project to which it pertained and was rendered largely inaccessible to anyone who might wish to use it. Unsurprisingly, the vast majority of 'records' were never transferred and continued to reside within the online service.

Keeping up with insatiable user demand

Though the new officially sanctioned suite of online applications was greeted as a huge step forward by the majority of users, it was not, of course, without its own limitations. Though perfectly adept at creating and storing the standard range of 'office' formats, it was less able to cope effectively with more specialist media. Many staff already had YouTube and Flickr accounts for their private use and often preferred to continue to use the services they were familiar with to store the totality of the multimedia files they created – including those at work.

A significant number of staff – well respected experts in their field – had long been keen bloggers, using their blogs to write on a range of professional and personal issues. The role these people play for the organization is only one facet of their professional life: many sit on several advisory panels or are members of professional societies and their blog posts tend to incorporate a mixture of all of these. Though the organization now provides its own in-house blogging service for those whose blogging is directly in support of the organization's activities, it has been unable to convince these more established and entrenched bloggers that they should cease their current blogs and start afresh within the technical and editorial boundaries set by the company.

Boundless potential

As a consultancy company and provider of professional services to other organizations, the quality and accuracy of the data the business holds about its clients (and potential clients) are critical. Buoyed by the success of their other forays into externally hosted Web 2.0 solutions, the company decided to implement its own commercially hosted Customer Relationship Management (CRM) system. Pursuing an open-source, Web 2.0 based solution soon yielded results; rather than pay for functionality they did not need, they were able to tailor it exactly to their own requirements. This included being able to create 'mash ups' (see page 100) between the CRM and staff members' social networking accounts; and allowing the company (where permitted by staff) to harness the invaluable intelligence offered through its users' Facebook and Linkedin activities. Further mash ups were created which combined the CRM with Google Maps and Satellite Navigation Systems to automatically provide directions and the required commercial information to sales staff prior to making a site visit. Meanwhile, RSS feeds ensured that the content of the CRM was automatically updated whenever a news story about a client was published anywhere on the web.

Determined not to rest on its laurels or fall behind the pace of technology again, the company is now actively pursing a presence in the virtual world of Second Life. It is still early days, but with many of its clients already buying their own Second Life islands, it sees this as a natural next stage for its commercial development. Some staff have already made potentially useful contacts while in Second Life, with some even resulting in subsequent real world business. It has also been suggested that providing professional services to clients *within* Second Life itself, to enable them to take advantage of the commercial opportunities it offers, could well represent a significant future growth area.

The organization has come along way in a few short years. Its infrastructure is now unrecognizable from the contained and centrally controlled environment of five years ago. Indeed, it could be said that it no longer has an infrastructure of its own, at least not in the physical sense of servers, local area networks and client applications. It still has information and records aplenty – far more so than ever before – and their importance to the organization has never been so manifest. At the moment it seems a limitless land of opportunity and potential, but could it also represent a Pandora's Box?

It is of course, a hypothetical scenario and an extreme one at that. There are a hundred different reasons why many organizations would never choose to go down this path. I, for one, do not fancy ever being a passenger in a plane built according to a specification produced by volunteer contributors to a wiki. It is no accident that I chose a scenario where the organization concerned had information at its core, but not as part of a complex manufacturing, engineering or development process. Yet, conversely, there is no reason why such companies should not discover echoes of at least some of the trends outlined in this chapter, indeed there are some leading research and development and manufacturing companies such as Procter and Gamble, and L'Oréal which are already taking steps in this direction.[1]

What I have tried to do in this chapter is to bring together the trends and technology of Web 2.0, which we have previously examined in the abstract, and demonstrate how they could conceivably come together and operate within an organizational context. Also, to show how organizations may find themselves having arrived at a place not too dissimilar to this via a series of small, logically progressive steps – rather than assuming that such a radical change of direction would, by necessity, require a deliberate, profound and considered change of strategy.

Although this may be a fictional account of a future scenario, we should resist the temptation to dismiss it as sheer speculation or science fiction. At the time of writing (October 2007) there is already clear evidence emerging that a range of diverse organizations are beginning to experience the effects of the rise of Web 2.0 and Office 2.0. It could be the announcement by Trinity College Dublin that they are to outsource their student e-mail service to Google Mail, or public statements to the same effect by General Electric or the Spanish police service that they are switching to Google Apps. Alternatively, it could be the growing use of Facebook by politicians as part of their election weaponry, or the prevalence of embedded YouTube clips in organizational websites.

The pace of change is bound to be hard to predict and likely to differ from sector to sector and organization to organization, but it *is* coming – and we ignore it at our peril. The key question that remains, as far as the priorities of this book are concerned, is where the principles and interests of records management fit into this picture? The records manager made only a fleeting and inconsequential appearance in this chapter, pushed to the sidelines by the pace of change and seemingly marginalized by the relentless push to utilize, rather than manage, information. Perhaps within this scenario he or she too would have shortly found their role outsourced to an external provider, able to provide an ongoing document storage and delivery service for less than the cost of continuing to provide this in house. The remainder of this book will now explore whether such increasing marginalization is indeed to be our professional lot, or whether records management can be successfully rethought for the Web 2.0 world.

Note

1 www.google.com/a/help/intl/en-GB/admins/customers.html
   #utm_source=hpp_lp&utm_medium=et&utm_campaign=en-GB
   [accessed 12 October 2007].

PART 2

Is records management no longer fit for purpose?

CHAPTER 5

The need for critical professional self-examination

Questions addressed in this chapter

- Should we be more willing to rigorously and critically self-examine our established methodologies?
- Are the ways in which we seek to address issues such as e-mail management and compliance with the Freedom of Information Act really fit for purpose?

The importance of continued professional reinvention

Many of the principles that underpin established records management theory were formulated in, and for, another age. As the preceding chapters have illustrated, I would argue that the degree and pace of change is now such that serious questions must be asked regarding the continued validity of much of our approach – at least when it comes to how we manage the kinds of information created within the Web 2.0 world. Historically, such a process of critical self-examination does not seem to be something that we, as a profession, are particularly good at doing. Other (though admittedly not comparable) professions, such as medicine, are continually having to review, reflect and reinvent the way in which procedures are performed, both in response to the opportunities offered by new technology, but also as our understanding of the human body evolves. A strong research base, rigorous continuing professional development and continual and heavily policed professional and public scrutiny, all help to continually push boundaries, to question orthodoxy and to innovate. Even less specialist areas such as manufacturing, retail and the media find themselves forced into a continual process of professional renewal that requires them to accept and even embrace change and to try to turn it to their advantage.

Can the same be said of the records management profession? The reflex response will inevitably be to leap to our own defence and to claim that we are, indeed, a proactive, vibrant professional community that is constantly reinventing itself, its tools and its techniques to cope with changing times; but is this really the case? Approaches to record retention and appraisal will be covered in detail in a later chapter, but for now it serves to point to the fact that the way in which we think about and practise our retention schedules has not, in essence, changed for the best part of half a century. If it were simply a case of 'if it ain't broken don't fix it' this would be fine, but in reality I fear it is more a case of 'we know it's broken but don't know how to fix it'. Think about our contribution to the management of e-mail, for example. If we were to be brutally honest with ourselves, we would be forced to admit that our impact in this arena has been marginal at best; likewise the management of websites, the contents of databases and the role we are playing in critical emerging fields, such as digital preservation. Naturally, there are pockets of good practice and areas where records managers are making invaluable contributions to these fields, but this does not seem to have led the profession as a whole on to new levels and to a wider consideration of whether management of such new media can really be accommodated within the existing canon of records management theory.

The gulf between theory and practice

To date, our approach to the management of e-mail is probably the best example of this. We are keen to remind users that e-mail can be a record and should be treated as such, but when reading the literature and attending conferences, the only approach usually heard in terms of enabling this is to implement an EDRM (Electronic Document and Records Management) system and ask users to transfer any e-mails they consider to be a record to it. Such an approach pays no attention to the nature of e-mail as a format, the volume of e-mails staff are routinely expected to deal with, or established user behaviour when sending and receiving them. It is a 'round' solution for a 'square' problem and, unsurprisingly, seldom works, and yet, because it is a 'solution' that is consistent with the principles of records management, we seem content to continue to promote this approach, seemingly blind to the fact that it has virtually no meaningful impact on the way staff manage e-mail.

Even in those areas that records managers in the UK would be quick to seize on as 'our territory' and a professional success story, such as compliance with the Freedom of Information Act (2000) (FOI), we seem to be happy to claim the credit while conveniently ignoring some fundamental challenges to our notion of records management, which accompanies it. Many UK records managers have become recognized experts in this legislation within their organization. They were rightfully quick to recognize compliance with the Act as largely a records management issue and to build up a detailed knowledge of the legislation that would put most lawyers to shame. Even now, some eight years after the passing of the Act, and more than three years after its full implementation, there are endless conferences and workshops run by, and for, records managers about this topic. Scores of new posts have been created in the public sector and many new records management projects established as a result – all of which is positive and to be welcomed. And yet, at the same time, it is questionable whether the types of solutions we have been striving for and promising to deliver are actually fit for purpose.

There has been no debate about how *records* management can cope with a Freedom of *Information* Act. Records management is selective; it only concerns itself with the wheat – that small percentage of an organization's information holdings that contain the properties and evidential weight required to give it the status of a record – and ignores the chaff of 'information'. But under a Freedom of Information regime such distinctions are rendered largely irrelevant. *Every* piece of information, regardless of how trivial or ephemeral it may be, is covered, can be requested and needs to be disclosed. It is unlikely that the recipient will care whether it has been classified as a record or not, so long as it provides the content they are seeking access to. Depending on the circumstances, the comment written in a jotting pad, the scribble on a Post-it note or the hastily composed e-mail, may prove of equal or even greater relevance to the requester than the approved minutes of a meeting, financial report or correspondence file.

Surely, on reading the text of the legislation back in 2000, one of our first professional responses should have been to realize that the logic underpinning FOI explodes the required scope of any public sector 'records management' programme to potentially encompass *any* piece of recorded information within the organization. How would we know what information was being created? How would we manage retention across the entire organization, rather than across a few record series? What would this mean in terms of the traditional priority we have given to records over information? Even the Section 46 Code of Practice on the management of records under FOI,[1] issued by the UK Lord Chancellor, does not address these issues, instead choosing to promote a 'text book' description of a traditional records management programme, with little or no discussion of its fitness for this purpose. Even after eight years such fundamental and challenging questions are rarely, if ever, raised.

As I hope to have demonstrated in the preceding chapters, this will shortly no longer be an option, thanks to the unprecedented nature of the technological and social change occurring around us. If our only response to such change is to trot out the same solutions and techniques, without consideration of their fitness for purpose, we will simply be overtaken by events and consigned to the history books. In the next few chapters we shall consider the essential characteristics of records management as traditionally practised and the pressures which, if not already here, will shortly be brought to bear upon them.

Note

1   www.dca.gov.uk/foi/reference/imprep/codemanrec.htm [accessed 2 March 2008].

CHAPTER 6

'Not all information sources are records . . .'

Questions addressed in this chapter

- What are the pros and cons of our deliberate focus on managing *records*?
- What are the dangers implicit in our reluctance to embrace change?
- Why are all information sources potentially now as valuable and powerful as records and worthy of equal consideration?

The inherent value of records

As any student of archives or records management will tell you, while all records are information, not all information sources are records. In the past there have been sound and defensible reasons for making this distinction. Records were self-evidently more important than information thanks to their evidential qualities. Records are what prove what you did, why you did it and what results it had. They are what lawyers, accountants and auditors want to see, because of the guarantees of quality and accuracy that go hand in glove with their status as 'records' – a status ensured through our insistence on adherence to standards of content, context and structure and qualities of authenticity, completeness, reliability and fixity.

These characteristics deservedly set the bar high and allowed records managers to focus on the subset of the information that met these criteria and could, therefore, be justly described as records. Formalized business processes helped create further clear blue water between information and records, with well established and unbending procedures for the generation of the minutes of meetings, memoranda and other business communications. In the pre-PC era, even the physical format of records was closely controlled, such as with the account book or the memo. Finally, the strictures imposed by file registry systems and the concept of the registered file ensured that records were routinely identified and logged even before their creation.

The consequences of our focus on records

Records management has, thus, long been defined by the narrowness of its focus. This is not a criticism, simply an acknowledgement that the profession emerged and developed to manage a very specific type of information and did not concern itself with the broader picture of information creation and use. Indeed, for many decades, this selectivity has been at the core of our professional strength and has hitherto served us well. By ring-fencing our scope we were able to produce a far more coherent and detailed set of professional principles than would otherwise have been the case. Ask a group of information or knowledge managers what the unifying theory is that underpins their work and they will give you a dozen different answers. Ask a group of records managers the same question and they will, by and large, answer with one voice.

Another, unintended, by-product of the narrowness of our focus has been to enable records management to continue to steer its course largely untroubled by organizational and technical change. As the range, complexity and volume of information platforms have increased in recent years, so we have been able to continue with our traditional activities, safe in the knowledge that, interesting as they may be, they do not create *records* and are not, therefore, our responsibility. We have already discussed some examples of this in terms of our professional response (or lack of) to the rise of the internet. To varying degrees, the same could be said about e-mail, instant messaging, research data, relational databases and line of business applications and now, of course, Web 2.0. All of these examples do, in some shape or form, have the capacity to create records, but somehow this has largely gone unnoticed. Rather than trying to push our professional relevance to each of these new technical trends at every possible opportunity, we seem to have done our best to run the other way.

Instead we leave the design, implementation and management of our databases to the IT team. We cling to the fact that the vast majority of e-mail and instant messages are not records, so we can focus only on the fractional percentage that are and ignore the rest. And we tie ourselves in knots by claiming responsibility for hardcopy staff files, yet largely ignoring the presence of the new HR system. This selective vision has been great in enabling us to continue to focus on the task in hand and to carry on the work started by our predecessors. We get to continue to manage the same record series and to ensure an unbroken continuum of care and at the same time take comfort in the resilience of a professional methodology that we continue to rely on, despite the maelstrom of change which surrounds us . . . and therein lies the danger.

The dangers of being cocooned from change

To a large extent we have made ourselves immune from change, wrapped in a professional cocoon that enables us to take a 'business as usual' approach, regardless of the realities of the outside world. Of course, there is considerable merit in continuing to hold a steady course and it is in nobody's interests to be constantly swayed from one direction to the other like a dinghy in a storm. Records management has always prided itself on taking the long view and not being subverted by current trends or fads, and that is to our professional credit. It gives us the gravitas and credibility to be able to say with confidence that our organization's interests are safe in our hands. But that is not the same as choosing to ignore change altogether. Even the captain of an oil tanker, able to ride out the roughest of storms, still needs to be constantly scanning the horizon and ready to make appropriate adjustments to its course and speed in order to avoid obstacles and maintain safe progress.

Ignoring the unprecedented rise in the volume and diversity of information being created by our organizations, simply because they are not 'records', does us no favours. Not only does it place a ceiling on the possible extent of our professional growth and reach, it also exposes us to accusations that we are failing in our professional obligations, even within the relatively narrow terms in which we ourselves have described them.

Choosing to manage only records was not an arbitrary choice. It was not the same as our forebears deciding that we should only concern ourselves with documents housed in a green cover, or only those that were typed in blue ink. Our methodology deliberately focused on the management of records because half a century ago an organization's records were a substantial and easily identifiable percentage of its information and represented, without doubt, the most important percentage. I would argue that this logic no longer necessarily holds true.

The power and value of information

We have already seen how one piece of UK legislation, the Freedom of Information Act, makes no distinction between whether the information in question forms part of a formal record or not. So far as requesters are concerned, they are after a particular piece of knowledge and it is likely to matter little to them whether that knowledge happens to be found within the body of a formal record, a notepad, e-mail or Post-it note. The same applies to other legislation directly relating to the management of information, such as the UK's Data Protection Act (1998). When it comes to personal data held *electronically* there is no reason to consider whether the e-mail, database, or document it resides in is a record; the fact that it contains personal data is, alone, sufficient to determine its inclusion within the Act. Likewise, any legal discovery exercise is bound to include any information of relevance to the matter under investigation within its sweep, regardless of its status. This scenario does severe damage to our professional claims to be protecting the legal interests of our organization. After all, what is the point of ensuring that 20% of your organization's knowledge-base is being managed to a high, legally compliant standard if it completely ignores the other 80%? It is like installing a sturdy, deadlocked security door to deter intruders, but leaving a large gap in the wall beside it.

I mention a figure of 20% of an organization's information as being records, but this is of course a purely arbitrary figure. It is difficult to place any accurate figure on this either historically or currently and much will depend on interpretation. For example, if we were to measure the percentage of the organization's knowledge-base that falls under the remit of the records manager, I strongly suspect that we would find this figure has dropped significantly in the past decade. One only has to consider the gigabytes of data now held within the website, line of business applications, databases and content systems and routinely out of the sphere of influence of the records management programme to concede this point. And yet, if one were to measure the percentage of information which may play a role in protecting the organization's legal interests, that figure is likely to be far higher.

This is the context in which we must consider the impact of Web 2.0. For some of the content created within it, such as social networking or video clips, it may be questionable whether it meets the traditional definitions of what falls within the remit of the records manager; and yet, I would argue, it should. We could choose to have endless theoretical arguments about if and when a wiki becomes a record, but while we are standing by and doing so we risk being overtaken by events. The libellous comments written on the company blog are just as damaging to its reputation and legal interests as the same comments recorded within the minutes of a meeting. The evidence of falsified research data discussed via an instant message exchange will be seized upon by investigators and lawyers with just as much zeal as it would be if it had been discussed by e-mail or memo. Perhaps even an employee's social networking activity could be used as evidence against them, if it proved allegations of insider trading or industrial espionage. In these examples I have focused on the negative and on the potential of these new technologies to create and harbour evidence that may damage the organization's interests. For the past 50 years it has been the self-appointed role of records management to limit such risks, or preferably prevent them altogether. If this is to continue in the years to come we must acknowledge that these same threats now come in different guises. The broadening of our scope that I am advocating does not mean taking on new roles, simply continuing to do the one we have already chosen for ourselves.

With other branches of Web 2.0, especially those relating to collaborative editing tools, the case for their evidential potential is even more clear cut. Staff who use Google Docs and the like to create, edit and share textual content are most certainly creating potential records. They may be doing this in ways that challenge our assumptions and undermine our methodologies but this is our problem, not theirs. As with the referee in a football match, it is up to us to keep pace with the game to a sufficient level to enable us to officiate; we cannot simply ask the players to slow down just because we are unfit.

Ultimately, perhaps rather than continuing to consciously or subconsciously avoid responsibility for this broader pool of information, we should seek to embrace it. Perhaps it is at last time to ditch our mantra that 'not all information sources are records' and instead begin with the assumption that 'all information sources are potentially records' and to see where this takes us?

CHAPTER 7

The centralized command and control ethos

Questions addressed in this chapter

- Why isn't records management scalable?
- Why are records management tools often too generalized to meet our users' needs?
- What are the limitations of our existing approaches to resource discovery?
- Why is tagging more popular than adding metadata?
- Are we about to witness the decline of the general applicability of the classification scheme?
- If so, what can we replace it with?

Records management as a bottleneck

Records management, as traditionally practised, is not infinitely, nor even highly, scalable and this represents a significant barrier to its potential and influence. In fact, records management as a discipline is founded upon a very strong and entrenched 'command and control' ethos, largely stemming from the US corporate culture of the 1950s where it could be said that records management as a discipline was toughened and given added rigour. It assumes that decisions will be made at the centre by a small select group of people (or indeed a single person in the form of the records manager) and that these will then be applied, largely without question, by the general user base. This assumption is evident in just about every branch of records management theory and practice: from the formalization of a classification scheme and metadata schema, to decisions regarding which records should be destroyed and which retained.

This is not to say that the records manager acts as a dictator. If he or she is to stand any chance of success, it has long been recognized that such corporate standards must be arrived at in consultation with their user base. We have all experienced (perhaps from both sides) the finely honed new working practice that seemed to work brilliantly on the drawing board but quickly sank without trace when released into the real world because of a lack of consultation. The gulf between theory and practice can often be a large one. But even when changes are introduced after extensive consultation, much of our records management practice still acts as a significant bottleneck – and one that may prove unsustainable as we move into the Web 2.0 world.

Let us look at resource discovery as an example. Established theory states that only through a combination of file plan, centrally dictated naming standards and metadata schema can accurate and comprehensive retrieval be assured. But the investment in establishing such standards, and more significantly in keeping them up to date, is massive. The accepted wisdom is that adopting a functional approach to classification and file plan development reduces this burden (on the basis that an organization's functions are more stable than their administrative structures). This is undoubtedly true. The organization will almost certainly continue to recruit staff, manage appraisal and provide opportunities for staff development, for example, regardless of whether the department responsible is called Human Resources, Personnel or some other variation. But that is not the same as saying that functions are static; a file plan, even a function-based file plan, does require continual maintenance if it is to accurately reflect what is happening on the ground. The problem is that there is simply no way in which a single records manager (or even a small records management function) can keep pace with such change – at least not at the level of detail that is really required.

The records manager as jack of all trades, master of none

Having worked as a records manager within a highly technical and specialist organizational environment (a pharmaceutical research and development company) I have had first-hand experience of being the non-scientist trying in vain to understand complex changes in protocol within the drug discovery process. Of course, it wasn't necessary for me to understand every nuance, but I did need to know enough to appreciate what the differences I was being informed of would mean for the way in which we managed their records (and all too often worried that I was falling short of the mark in this regard). Those that truly understood the changes being enacted were, of course, the scientists themselves.

A similar pattern is emerging in the work I have been involved with within the UK Further and Higher Education sector for the past six years. We have been responsible for creating a generic business classification scheme and records retention schedule for use by practitioners within institutions.[1] These tools have been carefully researched and refined over a nine-year period, involving three extensive consultation and review processes. It is, indeed, a valuable and popular suite of resources that has saved many institutions a great deal of time and money by forming the basis of their own institutional classification schemes and retention schedules. And yet inevitably, despite this effort and their undoubted strengths, they are far from perfect. In fact, their flaws are inextricably linked to the flaws implicit within our current centralized approach to records management; that is that where these tools are most accurate and detailed is in relation to the corporate functions and activities that records managers know best. Where their coverage and level of detail are patchier is where they attempt to cover the areas of teaching and learning and research. Here, while they may appear to pass muster to the records manager, they fall short of what practitioners in this area would expect as a fully accurate and useful representation of the processes and activities that they participated in.

Why should this be so? Why haven't we been able to simply address these weak points if we know they exist? This can be put down to two main reasons: firstly, the records manager is a generalist and as such what is there already – despite what the specialist in this area may regard as significant omissions and flaws – may appear fit for their purpose; secondly, it is one thing for us to be aware that the flaws exist, but quite another for us to be in a position to eliminate them. Where possible, the research and consultation that informs these tools tries to involve specialists in the respective areas, but inevitably a records management project run by records managers on behalf of the records management community attracts mainly records management practitioners. It is far harder to find the appropriate routes into other specialist practitioner communities and then to find sufficient experts who are interested enough in records management to devote the time required to address its weak points. What emerges is, therefore, a tool which appears to work for the records manager, but not necessarily for the users.

Until recently this could have been dismissed as an unfortunate, but inevitable, fact of life: after all, records managers are only human.

They cannot hope to be experts in every area of operation within their organization – especially if it is involved in highly specialist activities, such as manufacturing, engineering or research. The best that could be hoped for was that the records manager would have a good overall *feel* for the business and would not be afraid to ask the right questions and to seek help when required. So long as what informed the records management programme was detailed and accurate enough to serve the purposes of managing records (i.e. that the classification scheme was broadly accurate and of reasonable detail) this would be sufficient – especially as when presented to the user it would often be done in terms of a corporate tool to help manage records for legal and regulatory reasons, rather than something that necessarily addressed the operational needs of the individual user.

But, with the rise of tools and techniques that allow individual content creators to manage their own information, this need not continue to be the case. The experience coming out of the Web 2.0 movement is that harnessing the wisdom of the crowd through informal uncontrolled tagging, arranged by folksonomies for example, is an equally effective and certainly more scalable approach.

Folksonomy vs taxonomy

At first glance, the concept of resource tagging based on folksonomies may seem synonymous with the concept of metadata based on taxonomy. After all, both fundamentally involve the same principle of attaching additional descriptive terms to information, principally for the purpose of resource discovery. The crucial difference, however, is that the traditional metadata schema is devised and controlled centrally via the records manager. By providing the user with a defined pick list from which to choose, we can be sure that all financial reports will be correctly and consistently defined as a

'Financial Report' and not variously as 'Financial Reports', 'Finance Reports', 'Accounts' or 'Budget Statements'. Unfortunately, any model which relies on a single (or small number) of gatekeepers inevitably places a very low limit on its flexibility and speed of response. For example, how many existing metadata schemas could also be used by their organization to describe the multimedia collections that they hold alongside their regular information holdings? Likewise the gigabytes of raw data produced on a daily basis in fast-moving, fluid research departments. The chances are that the only way in which something dictated centrally by the records manager is able to be applied with any degree of accuracy to such dynamic or diverse areas is for them to be pitched at such a high level ('images', 'mass spectroscopy data', etc.) as to be rendered largely worthless to their main user constituent.

The people who are best placed to determine and apply suitable descriptive terms to the information they create are those who create or receive it in the first place. They understand its contents, its significance and its part in the process; and of course they know the type and level of detail that they and their colleagues are most likely to require in order to find and make use of that resource in the future. It is true that the creator, or recipient, is no more omniscient than the records manager; indeed while subject specialists may understand the information in question from their own individual perspective and part in the process, they may be largely ignorant of what happens to it after they are finished with it – or indeed what wider organizational, legal or regulatory requirements may dictate its management. But what if the knowledge of the creator were combined with that of subsequent users and then further refined where necessary by the experience of the records manager? Might this accumulated wisdom not represent a step forward in producing management controls which meet the needs of creator, user *and* records manager? Such an approach represents our first glimpse of what records management might look like in the Web 2.0 world and will be explored as such in greater depth in Chapters 11 and 12.

The pluralism of the Web 2.0 world is also likely to bang another nail in the coffin of the concept of the metadata schema, chiefly due to the practical problems associated with how to apply a schema across multiple, unconnected and more than likely externally provided, technologies. How is the corporate schema to be applied to the posting of a user's blog created and hosted on Blogspot, or their photographic collection hosted on Flickr? Moreover, how will our often superficial, restrictive and most likely out-dated schemas compete with the in-house tagging systems that all Web 2.0 systems now include, or with pan-system social bookmarking services such as Del.ico.us?

In fact it seems totally paradoxical that at the same time that records managers are struggling to get the users of their systems to add even the merest and simplest of metadata from a predefined list, so there are whole services that are thriving thanks to their users' seemingly insatiable desire to voluntarily categorize and tag the information of interest to them, and to make their decisions known to the world. Of course, there is undoubtedly a spirited defence to be made regarding the virtues of preserving quality over quantity, but my fear is that it will soon be drowned out by sheer weight of numbers. The simple truth is that people love to tag but hate to add metadata. Why? Perhaps it is because the folksonomy is an expression of the individual user's ability to describe the world as they see it and in ways that make sense to them. They have the freedom to decide what tags to give something; these may be selected from a list of terms already used by their peers, or be ones they create themselves if nothing else appears to fit the bill. It is a creative process and one that reveals a lot about the personality of the tagger. Moreover, it is quick, instinctive and easy; it is also infinitely scalable and indeed becomes more useful and more accurate the greater the numbers involved. Services such as Del.icio.us also allow users to incorporate these tags into virtually every facet of their online lives, by enabling them to be seamlessly applied to the online information they value in both their work and private lives, creating a holistic view that neither depends on, nor creates, false boundaries between their different personas.

Applying metadata from a controlled taxonomy or schema devised by the records manager is none of these things. It is intrusive and impersonal; it restricts freedom of expression and forces the user to view the world through a stranger's eyes; and worse still, a stranger with very different priorities from their own. It seems to be an administrative chore, divorced from the process of creation or use and even to belong to another era where search engines were unable to read and catalogue free text. Its scalability will always be severely hampered by the centralized change control procedures required to ensure quality; and it will forever force users to compartmentalize their lives and maintain the distinction between work and domestic use of information that is elsewhere in decline.

The death of the classification scheme?

> The provision of systematic and consistent classification schemes across the organisation is an important part of a records manager's work. Ideally, a single classification scheme should be designed to encompass all the records of the organisation. Every record should have a known place in the scheme, and its relationship to records in other parts of the scheme should be fully documented. However, in a complex organisation this is a demanding task requiring considerable time and expertise.
>
> (Shepherd and Yeo, 2003, 75)

In the light of what we have learnt already about how the workplace may look in a few years' time, this statement outlining the established view of the role of the classification scheme raises some interesting issues. Certainly, since its earliest days, the concept of the classification of records according to a predefined set of rules has lain at the heart of professional practice. The notion that 'every record should have a known place in the scheme' provides strong echoes of the days of hard-copy records where, due to the laws of physics, a single hard-copy record could only reside in one physical place at a time and it was important to know where that place was. Of course, in the world of digital records this no longer need be the case, but it is interesting to witness how we still feel compelled to conform to this principle. In part, this is undoubtedly due to the fact that the classification scheme is about far more than just resource discovery. Done correctly, it should also form the basis of many other aspects of the *management* of records. Areas of control such as those relating to access, security, retention and disposal can all, to varying degrees, be defined by a record's place within the classification scheme (assuming it is a functionally based scheme, where its place in the scheme reflects the business activity which created or used it). But in order for this to be the case the record can only have one true location within the classification scheme – regardless of whether we are talking about a single physical file or an electronic record.

The difficulties of applying a classification scheme within the Web 2.0 enabled office

Where the Web 2.0 world will really undermine the applicability of the classification scheme is in relation to the well established tenet that 'Ideally, a single classification scheme should be designed to encompass all the records of the organisation'. Let us briefly pause to remind ourselves of the new picture of information creation that is beginning to emerge. We are rapidly moving into a world where the volume of information an organization creates massively dwarfs the number of what we can best describe as traditional records (i.e. the types of record to be found in most classification schemes). As we have already established in previous chapters, much of this information is equally as valuable, or indeed dangerous, as our records, and logic would dictate, therefore, that it requires a similar level of management, but to my mind it is doubtful whether our classification schemes could ever be made to accommodate it.

Take the contents of the blog maintained by your organization's managing director for example. The blog will contain his or her thoughts and comments on a diverse range of topics: from the release of a new product, to the UK economy and the challenges posed by the release of a rival product. Where is this range of topics to fit within a subject-based classification scheme? And even within a scheme based on function there are substantial practical difficulties to be overcome, most notably how the blog is to be *physically* incorporated within the scheme. This promises to be especially problematic if (as is the case with most Web 2.0 systems) the technology hosting the blog is actually housed externally, via a third party.

Think back to our picture of the Office 2.0 world as described in Chapter 4. Here, we may have users storing their text documents on Google Docs, their video clips on YouTube and their presentations on SlideShare. These could be the product of the same function and/or relate to the same subject, but all are housed on separate unconnected systems. As such there is no intellectual or physical link between these disparate systems, or their content; the only common factor between them all is the individual user. There is no longer even the merest semblance of a corporately owned and maintained framework (such as a shared file store, or even the client–server architecture on which it is based) on which to 'hang' our classification scheme.

The logic underpinning a function-based classification scheme may still be sound, even in these very different circumstances. *In theory* (and I do deliberately stress the term *in theory*) the fact that the text file is stored in Google, the video clip in YouTube and the presentation in SlideShare is irrelevant: if they have all been created, or used, as part of the same process then this 'common ancestry' could and should still form the basis of their interdependency and be the key determinant of their management. In reality, the removal of the client–server architecture from the picture (an inevitable by-product of the logic of the adoption of Web 2.0 technologies) makes this virtually impossible to achieve – at least so far as records management practice is currently envisaged. Put simply, there no longer exists the organizational and technical foundations on which we currently rely.

We could, of course, still create our classification scheme and still dissect the functions, activities and transactions that define our organization; indeed there may well be other benefits and advantages in doing so. But, without the existence of the basic client–server architecture and in the current absence of any other underlying 'glue' with which to preserve the intellectual relationships inherent within physically dispersed digital objects, records management faces a real problem in the very near future.

At the beginning of this chapter we identified how the concepts of tagging, folksonomies and social bookmarking appear to address some of the shortcomings and limitations of applying traditional metadata schemas. Could tagging et al. offer similar potential in this regard too, not only in relation to resource discovery but as the basis of an alternative management tool? This is an idea which will be explored in further detail in later chapters; for now it is sufficient to identify the concept as one of promise – for what is a social bookmarking service such as Del.icio.us, if not a facility for 'over-laying' a common logic over disparate and otherwise unconnected web-based resources?

Problems of scalability

From the Shepherd and Yeo extract quoted earlier in this chapter, it seems as though the limitations of the classification scheme as a viable records management tool are already becoming evident – even when assessing it within its own currently accepted terms. The admission that 'in a complex organisation this [designing and fully documenting a comprehensive classification scheme] is a demanding task requiring considerable time and expertise' is a telling one. As our organizations become ever more large and complex and as the volume and diversity of information- and record-creating systems increase, so these limitations will become more and more apparent. Once again, we must accept that a core part of traditional records management practice isn't sufficiently scalable to deal with the demands being placed upon it. All the time the creation and maintenance of the classification scheme is the responsibility of the records manager, its ability to meet these challenges is bound to be fundamentally weakened. If it is to become more than simply a tool for the records manager's convenience and actually influence the behaviour of users, it requires a breadth and depth of knowledge that is virtually impossible for any one person to achieve. Furthermore, the current centralized model revolving almost solely around the records manager risks creating an unacceptable and unavoidable bottleneck in the process. It is too dependent on the skills, character and availability of an individual (or small team). And as just one activity, among the broad suite of tasks facing the records manager each day, the amount of time and resource that he or she is able to devote to it will almost always inevitably be less than it demands.

Could it be that, once again, harnessing the wisdom of the crowd in ways that support the objectives of the records manager could represent a viable alternative? It would require us to take a step back and release our grip on what we have traditionally considered to be our domain, but the advantages in terms of infinite scalability and the liberation of the expertise to be found within the user base may well outweigh these concerns – if we are bold enough to take the leap.

Reference

Shepherd, E. and Yeo. G. (2003) *Managing Records: a handbook of principles and practice*, Facet Publishing.

Note

1   www.jiscinfonet.ac.uk/partnerships/records-retention-he [accessed 12 February 2008].

CHAPTER 8

'Regardless of format . . .'

Questions addressed in this chapter

- Was there ever any merit in attempting to manage records 'regardless of their format'?
- Will Office 2.0 inevitably lead to format-specific information silos?
- What are the implications of the removal of a common storage facility within the Office 2.0 environment?
- Does the emergence of integrated Office 2.0 suites offer a potential new platform for management?

Did the concept of management 'regardless of format' ever really make sense?

It has long been an accepted truism of records management that we manage records according to their content and regardless of their format. It would have been nonsense to believe that the access or retention requirements of a record differed, simply because a version happened to be held on microfilm while another version covering the same content existed as a paper record. In this scenario, the format of the record is immaterial and from the management perspective it is the content that counts.

Certainly, when I was training to be a records manager a decade or so ago, the notion of management *regardless of format* was well and truly in vogue as a central plank of our approach to the management of electronic records. During the mid-1990s users were often likely to see the electronic version of their record as being somehow very different and even divorced entirely from its paper counterpart, which was clearly an unwelcome and unhelpful development. Our own professional perspective also risked being warped by the many and varied technical challenges posed by new electronic media, to the point where consideration of its content seemed almost an afterthought, with the focus very much on file formats, media instability and preservation of the bit stream. It must also be said that a concentration on content made life easier for members of the archive and records management professions. By retaining this sole focus on content, these professions were able to largely ignore the very real technical and scientific challenges posed by the need to manage the physical format of records, whether this be the specific storage requirements for magnetic media, the complexities of dealing with audio-visual content, or the science behind techniques for the mass de-acidification of late 19th century paper – all of which have been largely left to other professions to resolve. The mantra that we should consider and manage records according to their content and regardless of their format was a clear, succinct and persuasive argument and did much to ensure a continued sense of proportion and balance through these changing times.

Of course, as with much of life, in reality things are never quite that black and white. Although a handy catch phrase, the notion of a management approach which applied consistently, 'regardless of format', did conveniently gloss over some important changes and differences in approach, enforced by differences in format. This could be something as simple as the different ideal storage conditions for microfilm as opposed to paper; or in the digital world the need to capture additional metadata, such as native software and version number, in order to aid future preservation activity. There may also have been a need to allow technical staff to access the digital version in a way that would not have been necessary with the paper copy. These were all changes in management practice (albeit relatively minor) imposed by the need to consider a record's non-paper-based format. So perhaps we must acknowledge that, despite the soundness of its logic and the overall impact it has long had, management of records regardless of format was never actually the universal truth we may have liked to pretend it to be.

Even now that creating and managing electronic records has well and truly been absorbed into the mainstream, this is still a message that we feel compelled to repeat. This is most obvious in our approach to the treatment of e-mail. The argument usually put forward is that we don't separate our text documents from our spreadsheets and our presentations, so why do users store and manage their e-mail records separately in the silos that are their individual e-mail accounts? Instead, we argue, we should treat e-mail records as we would any other type of record and alongside the other records to which their subject matter relates. We all know that information silos are *a bad thing*: vital pieces of the picture may be overlooked, they may be managed inconsistently and they may fall outside whatever corporate management mechanisms have been decreed for records relating to that particular topic.

All of this is undoubtedly true, but still users continue to store the vast majority of their e-mails within their e-mail accounts, regardless of their relative 'recordness' and of our instructions to the contrary; and worse still this is a trend which is likely to increase dramatically in the Web 2.0 world, whether we like it or not.

A world of silos

Once again, we must think about the way in which our organizations are likely to evolve with the growth of Web 2.0 and Office 2.0 technologies. For, as we have already seen, one of the most distinctive defining features of this world is the proliferation of separate, often unconnected and largely externally hosted systems – every one a potential information silo in its own right. Worse still, the very raison d'être for many of these systems is their specialism in creating, manipulating and storing information of a certain specific format. Flickr has evolved solely to store, manage and provide access to photographs, as have YouTube and Video Clips. There is no facility for the user to also upload a series of text files or the like relating to their videos. It is this specialism that has propelled them to market dominance as they have been able to channel all their development activity and creativity to solving the problems posed by content stored in the format that their particular system manages.

While Flickr and YouTube may spring to mind as the most obvious examples, the same is also true of most Office 2.0 applications. When it comes to word processing systems you can choose from Buzzword[1] or Ebiwrite,[2] for working with spreadsheets you might select Num Sum,[3] Sheetster™[4] or wikiCalc®,[5] or for presentations plump for Scooch,[6] SlideShare[7] or Spresent.[8] In truth, I could have chosen at least a dozen systems as examples for each of these, but the key point is that the user has little choice in this new world, other than to store their text documents in one place, their spreadsheets in another and their presentations in yet another – regardless of the commonality of their content. The plus side for the user is that each of these systems is a specialist in what it does; the negative side for the records manager is that this is records management by format and regardless of content. For the user it is no longer necessary for all their eggs to be kept in one generic basket; they can now have a different, specialist basket for each type of 'egg' they produce.

Interestingly, it may also be that there are some advantages for the records manager too, especially in terms of the long-term management of electronic records. Although a detailed treatment of the complex subject of digital preservation falls outside the remit of this book, suffice it to say here that the preservation requirements of a digital photograph are likely to differ substantially from those of, say, a database, text document or web page. As such, a degree of management by format (as well as content) is already a steadily growing requirement of many records management programmes. Work such as the excellent PRONOM[9] registry of file formats, software products and other technical components founded by David Ryan and colleagues at The National Archives in 2002 is testament to this new need to manage content *inclusively*, rather than *regardless of* format (Darlington, 2003).

The decline of the common underlying storage facility

Exacerbating the trend towards increased heterogeneity is the fact that Office 2.0 systems are based on a fundamentally different model to existing desktop applications. Office 2.0 systems typically combine both the application itself *and* the mechanism for storing the content created within one indivisible system; there is no assumption of a separate, common storage area as there is in the desktop world. Users may create documents in Microsoft Word, but they do not store them in Word and the same is true for all other desktop applications. Microsoft Word and its brethren rely upon the presence of a separate storage facility that is common across all such applications. This storage facility could be a shared file server, but equally could be an individual hard drive, or even a CD-ROM or USB memory device. The important thing is that in the pre-Office 2.0 world, the act of content creation has been distinct from the act of storage and it has been the existence of this common storage facility that has provided records managers with the platform they require in order to continue promoting an approach to records management based on content, not format. The question is, if this is no longer the case, where does this leave us?

Integrated Office 2.0 suites

Hope might be forthcoming in the guise of a growing number of integrated Office 2.0 product suites, which provide a range of standard office tools, and the ability to upload existing Office files, all within a single combined Web 2.0 service. Google Apps[10] is probably the best-known example of this at the moment. It provides online access to files of a wide variety of formats and combines this with a calendar, mail service and web editor among other tools. Others, however, such as Zoho,[11] take a similar approach and offer an entire online product suite, rather than just specific isolated applications.

Could the formation of a common shared web infrastructure (albeit a virtual one) offer the same potential framework for enabling continued management by content, rather than by format, even within the very different environment of Web 2.0? The difference is, of course, that this shared framework does not belong to us, or our organization, but belongs to, and is defined by, Google or Zoho or whoever. Would we always be reliant on them to enact any management controls, or might there be the possibility of organizations imposing their own management 'veneer' over the top of the hosted service by means of an additional records management service module? It's an interesting thought and one which will be explored in greater detail in Chapter 12.

References

Darlington, J. (2003) PRONOM – a practical online compendium of file formats, *RLG DigiNews*, **7** (5), http://digitalarchive.oclc.org/da/ViewObjectMain.jsp?fileid=0000070511:000006280930&reqid=67759#feature2 [accessed 13 February 2008].

Notes

1 www.buzzword.com/# [accessed 12 February 2008].
2 http://ebiwrite.com/home.html [accessed 12 February 2008].
3 http://numsum.com/ [accessed 12 February 2008].
4 www.sheetster.com/index.jsp [accessed 12 February 2008].
5 www.softwaregarden.com/products/wikicalc/ [accessed 12 February 2008].
6 http://scooch.gr0w.com/ [accessed 12 February 2008].
7 www.slideshare.net/ [accessed 12 February 2008].
8 www.spresent.com/v2/ [accessed 12 February 2008].
9 www.nationalarchives.gov.uk/pronom/ [accessed 12 February 2008].
10 www.google.com/a/help/intl/en/index.html [accessed 12 February 2008].
11 www.zoho.com/ [accessed 12 February 2008].

CHAPTER 9

Appraisal, retention and destruction

Questions addressed in this chapter

- What do we mean by the term 'appraisal'?
- What were the factors which led to the development of a rigorous approach to retention management?
- How can we be sure that future generations will not blame us for what we have chosen to discard?
- Does random selection offer a viable alternative to selective appraisal?
- Should we not just keep everything?

Definitions

The related (but not synonymous) professional disciplines of records appraisal, retention management and record disposal lie at the core of our professional identity, and represent the last aspects of established records management practice that I wish to consider in the light of the rise of Web 2.0. In many respects, it is this focus on the management criteria required by our records, and in particular our techniques for determining how long records can safely be retained, that most differentiates us from other branches of information management.

The concept of appraisal extends beyond just consideration of how long records should be retained. The process of appraisal extends to all other aspects of the management of records and may also equally be used to analyse and identify access and security requirements, preservation criteria, resource discovery and appropriate use. However, most commonly the term 'appraisal' is used as shorthand to describe and support decisions about retention and particularly to identify how long different types of record should be retained before they can be disposed of in a safe and controlled manner, and it is within this context that it will primarily be considered within this chapter.

The origins and traditional rationale for retention management

'Records, whether paper or digital, cannot all be retained indefinitely. Storage and maintenance over time is often expensive and, as the volume of records grows, access becomes slower and more difficult' (Shepherd and Yeo, 2003, 146). Such has been the orthodoxy which has driven records management as a whole, and appraisal in particular, since its inception – and with good reason. Records management evolved as the answer to a problem. The problem in question was how modern organizations coped with the rapidly growing volume of records they were creating. This growth was in part fuelled by the increasingly complex nature of organizational functions and the bureaucracies that serviced them. It was also driven and partly enabled by the introduction of new technologies designed to speed up office processes and to ease the creation and duplication of hard copy records. The increasing ease of duplication was especially important in this regard. From the spread of the typewriter in the early 20th century, through to the invention of Xerography-based copying techniques in the 1940s and particularly the automation of this technique in 1960 – all of these developments resulted in an ever increasing proliferation of paper within many offices. Suddenly it became easier for staff to retain their own copies of the information they might need rather than needing to access a centrally held 'master copy' and for drafts to be circulated far more widely and more regularly than would once have been the case. Since the 1980s, these trends have, of course, exploded to levels that would have been unimaginable to our professional forefathers thanks to the growth of the personal computer, shared networks and desktop printers.

Put simply, organizations needed a way of separating the wheat from the chaff, of knowing which records were important and which were not, and of being able to find those that were. A surfeit of physical records is not an easy thing to ignore. It fills desks and cupboards and even makes entire rooms or buildings unusable for more productive purposes. Even attempts to rationalize their storage by the creation of designated 'offline facilities' that take advantage of economies of scale, or by outsourcing the whole task to commercial storage companies, still lead to very real and obvious costs. But the cost of buying yet another filing cabinet or of renting a warehouse is not the only price to be paid. Searching through box after box of unsorted paper, along shelf after shelf of unlisted boxes is a thankless, wasteful and unproductive task. And even when appropriate controls are in place to enable the location of the required box and its contents, the physical processes of identifying and retrieving the required record is inevitably time-consuming, the more so the greater the volume of records held.

The creation of defined methodologies to enable organizations to appraise the value of the records they held and to identify which records it was safe to destroy had a clear and compelling business benefit. It was not, and never has been, an exact science and there have always been risks associated with it. The act of destruction is (or at least should be) an irrevocable process; as such there is no margin for error. Given the range of potential values associated with a record, the breadth of uses it may be required for, both now and in the future, and the list of stakeholders with a possible interest in its contents, the risk of a mistake occurring is high and the ramifications potentially significant.

Whatever approach is adopted, the act of permanently destroying information is always fraught with potential dangers. Jenkinson[1] himself acknowledged the risks implicit in appraisal and its inherent flaws when he admitted that 'there can be no absolutely safe criteria for elimination' (1956, 149). The appraiser can never be absolutely certain that the value (or lack of) that they have ascribed to a record will be shared by the wider world and especially by our descendants. Archives and record offices around the world are filled with items which at the time of their creation would have been considered largely trivial but which today represent a goldmine for the historian or researcher. It is no different today; for example, many would consider the plethora of websites offering 'quack' remedies for medical problems and cut-price pharmaceutical supplies to be of negligible value, especially when compared with the quality of the information contained within the websites of reputable research organizations such as the Wellcome Trust. But to the 22nd century historian researching popular distrust of the medical establishment in 21st century Western culture, such sites could prove invaluable.

The passage of time inevitably changes the filter through which we view our world and assess its priorities. For example, we are fortunate that the private notes of a few keen amateur naturalists from the 17th, 18th and 19th century have survived, giving us a useful, if less than empirical, means for assessing the climatic conditions of the time and its effect on nature and the seasons. It is only within the past few decades that the significance of such contemporary observations has increased far beyond that of mere curiosity value or literary merit to become an important source of comparative climate change data. With no 'crystal ball' available it is impossible for us to predict what current sources, among the countless terabytes we create each day, may prove invaluable to future generations in tackling the challenges they will inevitably face.

The concept of provenance, an idea well understood by all archivists, also adds a further element of complication and potential risk to the act of appraisal. It goes without saying that a notebook of random jottings, thoughts and musing in the hand of Charles Dickens will attract considerably more interest and be considered inherently far more valuable than a similar book containing the thoughts of John Smith, a nondescript contemporary of Dickens who has left no other mark on history. Consider in this light the hundreds of thousands of blogs being written as you read these words. The chances are that 99.9% of them are unlikely to ever prove of any lasting value – save as part of some future, wide-scale, attitudinal research project where access to a few, randomly selected, samples would prove useful. But just as historians today may dream of stumbling across the hitherto undiscovered diaries of Hitler, Shakespeare or Napoleon, so too the blog written today by the student who will goes on to change our world for the better (or worse) may equally yield invaluable and fascinating information. But, of course, we can never know which of our children will go on to become world leaders and global icons, thus leaving the records appraiser in an invidious position.

The pros and cons of random selection

All of the risks outlined above would equally apply, even if the act of appraisal could be carried out by some theoretical, fully automated system which completely removed the human element from the process. But, of course, no such system exists in the real world and there is no way of removing the human element. The closest we can perhaps come to this is by adopting a process of appraisal based purely on random selection. As already mentioned, randomly selecting a small sample of records to represent the flavour of the totality may well have an important role to play where the sheer quantity of source data, and the perceived uniformity of its value, make any form of value-based appraisal impossible. Random selection or sampling has long been a weapon within the archivist's armoury when it comes to dealing with large volumes of certain types of physical records, especially those generated by a consistent bureaucratic process with little obvious individual content value. It is also beginning to attract some attention as a possible alternative to what could be described as value-based appraisal techniques when dealing with digital records (Neumayer and Rauber, 2007).

Perhaps the main advantage cited for random selection is that it does avoid the bias, either conscious or subconscious, that is implicit in appraisal. 'In trying to keep the most important or most valuable content, appraisal actively favours mainstream values, whilst sub cultural influences are effectively eradicated' (Neumayer and Rauber, 2007, 1). The archivist, or records manager, may offer a level of professional detachment which cannot be matched by the record's original creator or owner, but they cannot escape the sociocultural values, norms and beliefs which they have been exposed to as part of their education and experience and which must inevitably colour their judgement to some degree.

Proponents of random selection also point to its scalability. There is no need to spend time reading and analysing the content of individual records, nor to attempt to understand the detail, nor even to ascribe an arbitrary value to the labyrinthine processes that created them. Moreover, the percentage of records selected can simply be adjusted as resources allow, in theory making it infinitely scalable, though there must come a point at which the percentage of records selected is so small as to no longer be considered even remotely representative. But, unfortunately, random selection is no universal panacea for many other reasons too: most importantly the way in which it almost casually disregards any consideration of the relative value of the information contained within individual records, or of the processes which created them.

Such an approach is unlikely to find favour with many record creators who have invested significant intellectual capital into the creation of the record, or with those who have contributed to the process that created it. The creators and users of information are not passive bystanders when it comes to appraisal, but in fact represent the first wave of the appraisal process. After all, the act of creation itself and the decisions regarding if, when and how a record should be created are, in themselves, not without their subjective element – nor are early decisions regarding its use. The treatment of e-mail is an excellent example of this. We, as records managers, may issue guidance regarding the general types of e-mail which might qualify as a record, but ultimately it is up to individual users to make the decision themselves and decide which messages to delete, which to keep locally and which to transfer to the record-keeping system. In doing so they are clearly playing an active role in the appraisal process and doing this not on the basis of random selection, but of value judgement – immediately weakening the argument of those proponents of random selection who point to it as the only path to achieving a totally objective, bias-free, version of history.

Nor is an approach based on random selection a viable proposition for most organizations, especially those working within highly regulated and litigious industries. Take the data produced as part of the pharmaceutical research and development process as an example. Regulatory bodies such as the Food and Drug Administration or the Department of Health are likely to take a dim view indeed of the company that has deleted pharmacological records relating to the efficacy of a drug currently on the market, simply because they were randomly selected for disposal. Instead, retention must be based on a complex combination of both the relative importance of the process that created the record, and consideration of the status of the product to which it relates (i.e. whether it made it to market, is still in production or has been withdrawn).

Finally, it is doubtful whether random selection offers a solution to the problems discussed earlier in this chapter regarding the difficulties in identifying and preserving the works of future leaders and icons *before* they achieve greatness. Of course, if we choose to randomly select and retain 5% of blogs, for example (and it is perhaps also worth noting that the very act of deciding what percentage of any particular type of record to retain is, in itself, a subjective one), there is a 5% chance of the blog of a future Winston Churchill or Nelson Mandela being preserved. But such small odds are hardly reassuring and offer no means by which we can use any possible hint of future greatness, such as obvious early talent or the respect of contemporary peers, as an aid to informed selection.

With all these seemingly intractable problems, compromises and dangers involved in the process of appraisal – apparently regardless of how it is carried out – it naturally begs the question as to whether we would be better off by simply avoiding the task altogether. For Jenkinson it was seen as an inevitably flawed, but ultimately necessary, evil required when dealing with the 'intolerable quantity of documents accumulated by modern administrations' (1956, 149). But is this still really the case? Rather than simply assuming that we must find ways of destroying information, shouldn't we at least explore whether in this new world of cheap, and apparently near infinite, electronic storage capacity the same fundamental drivers for appraisal and retention management still apply?

Why not keep everything?

As the reader of this book will no doubt already have noticed, I am a firm believer in the need to question, rather than simply accept, the continued validity of some of the core principles of records management theory and practice. After the passage of more than fifty years and a revolution in the way in which our organizations create and use information, this seems to me to be a perfectly legitimate, and indeed necessary, course of action. If such tenets really do deserve to continue to define how we apply records management in the 21st century they should be able to stand up to such scrutiny; alternatively, if they don't, it is important that we recognize and acknowledge this and take the appropriate steps required to compensate for it.

As we have already seen in this chapter, there can be no tenet so holy to the records manager than the assumption that the organization must be selective in what information it chooses to retain. Regardless of the approach to selection and appraisal chosen, the underlying assumption is always the same: we can't keep everything, therefore we need methodologies to help us determine in as objective a way as possible what to keep and what it is safe to destroy. Half a century ago this was indeed an undeniable fact. Records held on paper have a physical footprint and resulted in direct costs associated with their storage. As the means to produce paper records became ever more effective, so it did indeed, to all intents and purposes, become an impossibility to retain it all. The alternative was to accept huge and increasing storage costs and a decreasing ability to locate and retrieve the information required. Reducing the physical footprint of paper records by transferring them to microfilm or microfiche may have helped reduce these costs and increased the available storage capacity, but was itself relatively costly, was far from infinitely scalable and also had its own problems in terms of required storage conditions and speed of access.

But we now live in a very different world, where such assumptions about the physicality of records need no longer apply. The ubiquity of digital information and the enormous storage capacity of digital media mean that a whole new set of options and possibilities are open to us. The question is whether such options now extend so far that they do actually offer us the possibility of retaining everything that our organizations and their staff create; and if so whether this should now be our goal. At the very least, we should not simply dismiss this opportunity out of hand without first considering the pros and cons of this as an objective and then considering the practical problems that may stand in the way.

Certainly, many of the key players in the IT industry seem to see unlimited digital storage as representing a great step forward for mankind and one of the goals that the industry should be striving to achieve. We have already seen evidence of this in Chapter 1 and the concept of a 'future without limits'[2] thanks to the promise of apparently limitless digital storage.

There can be little doubt that digital storage does remove many of the obstacles to universal retention that were an unavoidable fact of life when dealing with physical records. First and foremost is, of course, the vast, almost unimaginable volume of data that can now be retained in a small physical space and at apparently little cost. One need only imagine how much space it would take to store the contents of the average file server if they were printed to paper to appreciate the profound implications of our ability to condense the storage of information; and yet even this is as nothing compared with the volume of information available via the internet free of charge and with no storage overheads to the end user. Perhaps the most obvious example of this difference is the comparison between the cost of ownership (both in terms of purchasing and storage) of a complete run of *Encyclopaedia Britannica* compared with Wikipedia. This is not to imply that their content, accuracy or value are equal but, so far as many end users are concerned, they would appear to value the accessibility and currency of the latter over the authoritativeness of the former. With many Web 2.0 and Office 2.0 service providers offering virtually limitless storage capacity for no charge this promises to free organizations from the last remaining shackles of storage overheads by doing away with the need for their own racks of servers, back-up facilities, uninterruptable power supplies and the like.

Secondly, we now have the tools at our disposal to enable us to find the required needle of information in the digital haystack of limitless storage in a way far beyond the wildest dreams of our forebears. There is no need for us to consider the intellectual or physical order of the information we hold, we do not even need to artificially add descriptive metadata to each item any more. It is perfectly conceivable for us to simply create the information we require and to rely on search engine technology to automatically index every word and analyse every link. Should that not be sufficient there are also a number of other painless techniques we can adopt to further hone and polish our ability to retrieve the information we require and to have it delivered to our desks within seconds.

Largely as a result of these technical advances, we now live in a world defined by information storage; ours is now a culture in which size most definitely matters. Just take each new generation of iPod that hits our shops. Have you ever seen an improved ability to decide what tracks you want to delete quoted as a selling point? No. However, the fact that it now has a 16Gb memory, compared with the 8Gb available last year, or the 4Gb the previous year, most definitely is. Even other neat 'must have' features such as the ability to play video footage are only made possible thanks to the additional memory now available, while new user interfaces are designed to help ensure that we can continue to find the right song at the right time. The ultimate goal of being able to fit your entire music collection in your pocket on a device no bigger than a pack of cigarettes is almost here. You may not have listened to that *Best of Leo Sayer* album since you were nine years old, but why not add it anyway? It doesn't cost you anything, you have the spare space and who knows you may just feel the urge one day . . .

Whether we like it or not, the whole concept of selective retention and the deletion of data is now alien, not only to the IT industry, but to popular culture and the society in which we live. One aspect of the Web 2.0 revolution that may well increase this trend yet further is the mash up. Mash ups are combinations of data from more than one (online) source to achieve a novel 'value added' new data source. Popular examples at the moment include layering multiple additional data streams over a mapping service, such as Google Maps, to graphically illustrate interesting or useful geographical trends. The potential applications for this are literally endless and impossible to predict in advance. It could well be that what appears to be an old, unused and worthless data set, collected some years previously, could, when 'mashed' with other sources, now prove to be the missing piece of a vital puzzle. As a result, the concept that any individual piece of information has a finite and definable lifespan is severely weakened as there is no means of knowing the value it may play as part of an as yet unknown future combination of data.

Mash ups are very much in their infancy at the moment, but their prominence and use will only increase; after all by making use of existing research data and other information for new purposes, it is a far cheaper and quicker process than having to collect new data. It also represents another step in the direction of the personalization of IT. Mash ups allow the individual user to create their own view of the world according to the combinations of data that they are interested in. For example, when looking to move to a new area why not feed in all the instances of the particular leisure activities that you are keen on, the schools that cater for your child's age range and the areas with the lowest crime rates to produce a personalized map of your ideal places to live. The potential is endless, but all depend on the availability of existing information.

We must acknowledge that, regardless of whether we are right or wrong, our emphasis on selective retention now appears to be swimming against hugely powerful currents, and that at the moment we seem to be steadily falling further and further behind. Faced with the choice, our IT departments would rather spend money on buying a new server than spend the time and effort required to appraise and sort the contents of the existing one. And even with the growing recognition of climate change and the scarcity of natural resources, the drive of IT innovation is currently to continue to find cooler, larger and more effective storage technologies and not to focus on reducing the volume of information we store in the first place. Perhaps the ultimate expression of this trend is Google's recent relocation of one of its server farms to The Dalles in Oregon to enable it to access the massive amounts of electricity it requires from the local hydroelectric dam to run its server farms.

In view of this, perhaps now is the time to stand up and acknowledge that, thanks to these changes, we are working from the wrong starting point and basing our approach on a flawed assumption. Perhaps we should be ready to admit that keeping everything may now be an option, rather than simply dismissing it as either impossible or just plain undesirable, as has hitherto been our approach. After all, keeping everything would remove most, if not all, of the risks implicit in appraisal, as identified by Jenkinson and others. It would also be more in tune with the drive of popular culture, IT development and user behaviour (all of which we are dependent upon whether we like it or not). It provides us with the ability (in theory at least) to capture and record every facet of human culture and history, free from the imposition of value judgements, bias and quotas. As we have seen, the act of appraisal must always be a compromise and must always be a flawed process. Indeed, even by its founding fathers it was never viewed as the ideal, but simply as a necessary evil. It was required because it was previously impossible for us to entertain the idea of capturing and keeping everything; but now that this is seemingly within our grasp, perhaps the rationale for appraisal has finally run its course.

What about the smoking gun?

The first reaction of many when confronted with a proposal to keep everything will no doubt (and quite rightly) be scepticism as to whether this really is technically feasible, and this is a point to which we shall return shortly. The second reaction following close upon its heels is likely to be one of considerable concern, for the simple reason that many organizations are acutely aware that among their legitimate holdings of information may lurk the carelessly worded e-mail, the defamatory comment or the fraudulent document. Fear of the discovery of what is commonly referred to as 'the smoking gun' is often employed by the records management community as an essential driver for retention management, and one that is sure to get the ear of senior managers. The logic is simple: the less information an organization holds, the less the chance of such dangerous documentary evidence ever coming to light.

There have been numerous examples in recent years of organizations that have seen their reputation, and in some cases their business as a whole, left in tatters as a result of scandals caused by the discovery of records they wish had never seen the light of day. In the UK, the introduction of Freedom of Information legislation in 2005 has caused many a public sector manager to worry about what may need to be disclosed, should a request be received under the Act. The many exemptions contained within the Act should provide sufficient protection from the need to disclose legitimate but sensitive or otherwise confidential information. The concern is more likely to focus on information held by the organization (and therefore covered by the legislation), but held unofficially and potentially unlawfully: the e-mail containing a sexist joke about a colleague or defamatory remarks about a competitor; the memo attempting to cover up an embarrassing episode; the paper trail that reveals the perpetration of a deliberate, if not necessarily malicious, illegal act (such as an irregularity in a tendering process to benefit a favoured supplier, or the covering up of a breach of health and safety regulations).

As a profession we have grown accustomed to stating with some confidence that good records management is an essential element of ensuring high standards of corporate accountability and good governance. In the same breath we also proudly assert that records management and retention management in particular will help lessen the risk of discovery of the smoking gun and therefore help protect the organization's interests. But are these two statements really consistent? Surely when one considers the logic behind these arguments, rather than being seen as complementary, they should, in fact, be viewed as contradictory. Deliberately removing the smoking gun – destroying the e-mail or paper trail that proves a fraud or other crime has been committed – does not prevent it from happening, it merely prevents the perpetrator from being discovered. Indeed, it could be said to actually encourage malpractice by reducing the perceived likelihood of detection. Rather than records management as a tireless defender of good corporate management, this is records management as accessory after the fact. Yes, removing the evidence may help protect the organization's reputation and yes this may well be in the interests of the organization, but this is surely a morally dubious position for records management to take and hardly consistent with our claims to be an integral element of good corporate practice.

It therefore seems as though a strong logical argument could be made that keeping everything is the best possible means of ensuring good individual and corporate standards. After all, what better deterrent to the potential corporate criminal, or simply the careless and maverick e-mailer, than to know that every word they write is being kept centrally under close corporate control and will be available for inspection at any time. So, once again, we see further evidence of why some of the assumptions on which our tradition of appraisal and destruction are based should be subject to fresh scrutiny, rather than simply accepted without question as sacrosanct.

But keeping everything is not a panacea either

At first glance, it would seem as though life for the records manager would be far simpler in a world in which we agree to keep everything. In reality, however, not only would it just mean replacing one set of problems with a different (perhaps even more substantial) set, but there are also serious questions to be asked about whether it would ever be achievable in practice, even if desirable in theory.

Even though our capacity to store information has increased phenomenally over the past decade, this is not the same as saying that our capacity is infinite, or even that the current rate of growth is necessarily sustainable into the future. There must always be some theoretical limit to our storage capacity, even if set at an astronomically high level. Moore's Law may have been our guide since the 1960s, but many commentators suspect that we are now nearing the end of our ability to keep pace with the exponential rate of growth required. Very soon the inviolable laws of physics will dictate that it is simply impossible to cram ever more components into an ever smaller space. Improvements in the composition of the materials used may buy us some breathing space but will not provide a sustainable answer. Of course, it is possible that science may yet ride to the rescue by utilizing some hitherto unthought-of storage media based on light particles, chemical compounds or organic matter, but can we really afford to passively sit back, wait and hope?

Then, of course, there is the question of energy. Digital storage is a hungry beast and collectively consumes vast amounts of electricity. Surely to assume unlimited storage capacity is also to assume unlimited energy and reserves of the resources we currently rely on to provide it? This is not the place to discuss the pros and cons of the various approaches to filling the increasingly evident shortfall in the natural resources we currently rely on to provide our power. It suffices to say that energy is not the cheap, limitless and taken for granted commodity that we had grown used to assuming it to be and that there must one day be a limit to the number of hydro-electric dams that Google can tap into.

In fact, perhaps our historical and current attitudes towards energy consumption provide the most telling parallel to how popular opinion may develop regarding information storage. We are now living through the storage boom times: it's cheap, ubiquitous and seemingly inexhaustible. As such it can be used, abused and wasted without a second thought, just as oil was throughout much of the 20th century. But just as we are waking up to the fact that such a profligate attitude to the consumption of energy is not sustainable and is increasingly viewed as selfish and even immoral, so we may soon see a similar change of opinion regarding information storage. Yes, it may be possible for us to store and retain vast amounts of meaningless and ephemeral information, but just because we can does not necessarily mean that we should. Maybe at that point we will finally see the first iPods being promoted as much by their new functionality to manage their contents as their ability just to store them.

It is also possible to foresee a time when a combination of these factors – the end of Moore's Law, rising energy costs and a change in the public's attitude towards the environmental costs and ethics of storage – actually leads to a change in policy by existing storage service providers. As we have seen, many Web 2.0 and Office 2.0 companies currently offer their service free of charge, at least for the entry-level package. This has been necessary in order to achieve the participation of the crowd that their business model relies upon (with a large volume of 'foot fall' on the site attracting high returns from advertising). But if the changes outlined above do come to fruition, will they be forced to think again and start to impose some form of levy on all account holders based on the volume of content they hold? If so, we may well see a renewed focus within those organizations that have chosen to outsource their information storage on how to limit the volume of information they hold in a safe and managed manner.

Such a change may well force us to rethink the value we attach to certain types of information. In a world which assumes infinite 'free' storage it seems harmless, perhaps even advisable, to advocate the retention of everything – even the trivial and the ephemeral. Should these assumptions prove to be flawed, it will inevitably become far harder to make the case for keeping every spam e-mail and the like just in case there is some possible future niche research activity that could find them useful. Regardless of the criticisms of bias levelled at appraisal it is a simple fact of life that not all information is of equal value and that surely there must come a point at which the overheads associated with storage outweigh the value of its content.

Nor should we lose sight of the fact that the accumulation of such ephemera all acts as 'noise', drowning out the clarity with which we can identify and locate the information we actually need. Yes, there is value in serendipity and the chance of discovering the unpolished gem among the trivia, but it is a long shot. The more likely scenario is that despite the impressive resource discovery tools at our disposal the permanent retention of everything will simply serve to obscure, overwhelm and obstruct. Even with perfect retrieval tools we are still limited by the capacity of the human brain to absorb and process information and the danger of information overload is correspondingly high. It is possible to have access to *too much* information and as a result for the speed and quality of decision making to be damaged to almost the same extent as is risked by operating with a lack of reliable information.

Finally, when it comes to certain types of information, we must acknowledge that in Europe at least, there is no option to indefinitely retain *all* information. Principle 5 of the UK Data Protection Act 1998 states that 'Personal data processed for any purpose or purposes shall not be kept for longer than is necessary for that purpose or those purposes'.[3] This is not a limitation period, nor a recommended retention period that can be ignored or extended if required. It is, quite uniquely, a mandated obligation to actively destroy personal data when its specific function has been completed. The legal requirements surrounding the management of personal data are therefore incompatible with any carte blanche decision to retain all information, regardless of any theoretical advantages this may afford. Of course, it could be possible to identify personal information where it is held and introduce measures to manage it appropriately while still undertaking to keep the rest, but achieving this must inevitably mean introducing an element of appraisal and selection to all the information we hold, thus rendering the 'keep everything' argument fatally flawed.

If we do concede this point – and take into account the other problems we have identified in this section – we must surely find ourselves back at the conclusion that appraisal in some form, despite its flaws, still remains a necessary evil today just as it was in Jenkinson's time. The question this inevitably raises is whether our existing approach to appraisal is still fit for purpose and in particular whether it will be able to cope with the implications of a shift towards a Web 2.0 driven future.

References

Jenkinson, H. (1956) Modern Archives: some reflections, *Journal of the Society of Archivists*, **1**, 147–9, reprinted in Ellis, R. H. and Walne, P. (eds) (1980) *Selected Writings of Hilary Jenkinson*, Alan Sutton.

Neumayer, R. and Rauber, A. (2007) Why Appraisal is Not 'Utterly' Useless and Why It's Not the Way to Go Either: a provocative position paper (PPP), DigitalPreservationEurope, www.digitalpreservationeurope.eu/publications/appraisal_final. pdf [accessed 18 February 2008].

Shepherd, E. and Yeo, G. (2003) *Managing Records: a handbook of principles and practice*, Facet Publishing.

Notes

1 Sir (Charles) Hilary Jenkinson (1882–1961), Keeper of Public Records at the UK Public Records Office and an early influential thinker and author on archival theory.

2 http://ymailuk.com/blog1/2007/03/28/yahoo-mail-goes-to-infinity-and-beyond/ [accessed 20 September 2007].

3 www.opsi.gov.uk/acts/acts1998/ukpga_19980029_en_1.

CHAPTER 10

The problems with applying existing approaches to appraisal in the Web 2.0 world

Questions addressed in this chapter

- Why are our current appraisal techniques not scalable enough for use in a Web 2.0 environment?
- Why is it not enough to just consider the evidential significance of an information source when considering its value?
- How much can we expect from information creators and users during the appraisal process?

Appraisal theory and reality

Firstly, we must acknowledge that it is over-simplistic to assume that there currently exists just one universally accepted view of appraisal and retention management. In fact, as you would expect with a profession dealing with such a wide variety of record and information types within a broad spectrum of sectors and organizations, there is a considerable diversity of theoretical opinion and practical application. Such diversity is a healthy recognition of the fact that 'one size does not fit all', and is to be welcomed. It can, however, make for a confusing landscape, especially as it would be a mistake to assume that approaches to appraisal are necessarily clearly and cleanly defined. Theories merge and overlap and circumstance often dictates a pragmatic approach that includes elements of more than one methodology.

On a more general level, the one factor common to all approaches is the need to recognize the potential gulf between established theory and practical reality. It is often said that politicians believe that announcing the introduction of a new policy automatically equates to the successful implementation of that policy, whereas, in reality, there is often a considerable gulf between the two. Perhaps, the same could be said to apply to much of our thinking with regards to appraisal. Just because we have a well established theory does not mean that it really has the impact we might hope for in reality. Our approach to e-mail appraisal is a classic example of this. I have attended several conferences and events on this topic, full of earnest presentations from the podium about the importance of identifying and retaining only the small percentage of e-mails that count as records, and then have overheard the conversations over coffee where these same people admit that users within their organizations (sometimes even themselves) openly hoard countless .PST files full of thousands of e-mails . . .

As we have seen in the preceding chapters, the way information is now created and used has altered enormously in recent years and looks set to change out of all recognition in the near future. There is, clearly, still a need for organizations to appraise the information they create and keeping everything remains as problematic and even potentially unwelcome an approach today as it always was. In some highly regulated and controlled industries, appraisal and retention may still need to be carried out along the time-honoured lines of item-by-item, process-by-process analysis, but the focus of this book is primarily on how we manage the rest: the vast volumes of information that fall outside the traditional sphere of records management. Given what we have already discovered about the nature of records management in the Web 2.0 world I believe that appraisal methodologies as currently applied are likely to prove inadequate in dealing with these changes due to the following factors.

Scalability

The challenges posed by the volume and diversity of information being created in the Web 2.0 world have been a constant theme running through this book and their impact is likely to be most apparent when it comes to finding methods of appraisal that are scalable enough to cope. We have already established that appraisal is still required in this world, but it is appraisal on a scale the like of which we have never had to contemplate before.

This instantly discounts approaches such as the Grigg system (1954) established as part of the UK Public Records Act of 1952 and still influential in the appraisal of many UK public records. Grigg mandates a two-stage, item-by-item, appraisal of the file's contents: firstly to assess continuing operational need and secondly to determine any subsequent historical value.

Interestingly, the focus within Grigg is on departmental staff carrying out these reviews and not professional archival or records management staff. As such, it does offer a degree of scalability that is not shared by appraisal techniques relying heavily on the involvement of the individual records manager. It stands to reason that the creators and users of the file should be well placed to know and understand its contents, and to make at least a semi-informed decision regarding its operational value. There may, however, remain question marks as to their ability to appreciate the value of a particular file within the broader organizational perspective (i.e.

beyond their individual role and relationship with the item in question) and particularly their qualification to judge its historical value. But, regardless of these potential weaknesses, the underlying assumption of the involvement of the lay user in the appraisal process is an interesting one, and one which, as we shall see, may well prove relevant when establishing an appraisal methodology suitable for the Web 2.0 world – especially if that same technology may offer the potential to address some of these traditional shortcomings.

The other limitation of Grigg is another result of the manual basis on which it has previously had to be applied. Until very recently there has been no choice but for the contents of each file to be read (or at least 'skim-read') by the human eye in order to determine its subject matter and the relevance of its content. This was a time-consuming process and a hugely limiting constraint on its scalability. Given the volume of information we are now talking about, there is simply no way that appraisal can be carried out based on a reading of its contents by human eyes. It would be the equivalent of trying to index the entire contents of the world wide web manually, without the use of web crawlers and search engines. Thankfully, when it came to indexing the web we were able to invent automated tools to do the job for us; perhaps the same may yet prove possible for the process of appraisal.

Scope and detail

The assumption underpinning most organizations' appraisal activity, even if not explicitly stated, seems to be that it only applies to a small percentage of the information they hold; those that are very definitely core records. This is evident in the scope of most retention schedules, which, though comprehensive within their own terms of reference, often seem to ignore information or even records that are not text-based, are held in new technologies or whose pattern of use defies traditional definition. For example, few retention schedules seem to have found rigorous and objective ways of appraising the relative and changing value of photographs, even though the images in question may well have operational or evidential qualities and not just represent a historical record of an event.

Many retention schedules also struggle to span the divide between physical and digital records, even when they relate to the same function or subject area and despite the assumption of the 'regardless of format' mantra that we discussed earlier. For example, the retention schedule may well cover the staff personnel file and its contents but rarely encompasses the same data and related content as held on the personnel database. Of course, with the 'regardless of format' mantra in mind, we could just rely on the fact that whatever is determined for the physical manifestation of the record automatically applies to its digital counterpart, but this risks falling into the trap outlined earlier of mistaking words with deeds. Do the rules defined by the retention schedule really influence the way the database manages the information it contains, or do we just conveniently ignore the gulf between theory and practice in this regard? To be truly effective the contents of the retention schedule, and the management decisions it mandates, would have to be integrated within the design of the system itself, to enable the degree of automation required to make this work. Furthermore, it is likely that the database operates at a level of granularity far below that of the paper record. There will be identifiable individual fields within the database that perhaps require individual management decisions. A staff record held on a personnel database may comprise dozens, perhaps even hundreds, of such fields: each created and used for a specific purpose and each potentially having its own retention and appraisal requirements. How many times is such complexity ever reflected in the traditional retention schedule?

Databases are just one example of where our techniques for

managing appraisal have not kept pace with technical advances. By and large, the same is true for intranet and internet sites and the content management systems that drive them; equipment generating or measuring research data; line of business applications; digital asset management systems; and now, of course, wikis and blogs. As we have seen, the old arguments about whether such systems actually contain *records* are now largely meaningless. Their contents contain information that is of value to the organization and equally has the power to damage its interests if misused and thus should all be subject to the same levels of appraisal management as traditional records.

If many organizations struggle to apply their retention schedules in a dynamic and effective way to the systems they own, house and manage themselves, this of course raises the question of how they can ever cover information stored by external services over which they have no direct control, as is the case with many Web 2.0 applications.

Failure to adequately assess information value alongside evidential value

The archive and records management profession has not been blind to the limitations on scalability implicit in Grigg and other file-by-file based appraisal methodologies. In recent years the concept of *macro appraisal* has become increasingly attractive and the basis of many appraisal programmes required to cope with large volumes of records. Macro appraisal places far less emphasis on the need to read, review and assess the *contents* of records, preferring instead to focus on an understanding and assessment of the nature and relative value of the organizational function that created them. If we can quantify the importance of the function, so the argument goes, a similar value can automatically be applied to all of the records it creates, hence ensuring a far more scalable approach to appraisal.

The other main advantage to macro appraisal is the emphasis it places on an appreciation of a record's context. Contrary to Grigg and the like, macro appraisal forces the appraiser to primarily consider the record in terms of how it relates to the functions of the organization and its use by staff, thus creating a more comprehensive picture of the record's true status.

Macro appraisal has much to recommend it, particularly for those records created by one or more clearly defined processes, and records whose value is intrinsically linked to the process that created it. It may, however, be less relevant as an approach to the appraisal of Web 2.0 information. As we have seen, macro appraisal places little value on consideration of the content; while this may be fine for appraising the *evidential value* of records resulting from a clearly defined process, it is far less helpful when it comes to trying to define the *content value* of information, which even if created as the result of a clearly defined process (which may not always be the case), may subsequently be reused for many others. Photographs or other multimedia resources would be a good example of these limitations. Yes, a photograph is always taken for a reason, but that reason may not necessarily be linked to a specific business process; it could simply have been an image that a member of staff thought would be useful or relevant to something they are working on. Perhaps others may find it similarly useful both now and into the future, or perhaps they won't; or perhaps it will be useful for a limited amount of time but will quickly date and drop in value. Macro appraisal is of no use in this scenario, where the context is of little consequence; what counts is the content.

Macro appraisal is a tool for professionals and largely ignores the voice of the record creator and user; it is the process that is of interest, not the opinions of individuals. As we have seen, this is the quality that enables its scalability, but at what price? In Chapter 7 we discussed how the records manager may be far less qualified to understand the complex processes that create a record, than the people who use it on daily basis. It could be said that to base decisions regarding what records to keep largely, if not solely, on our own (perhaps mistaken or inadequate) understanding of the processes that created them, is a risky and even arrogant proposition and one that is unlikely to endear us to our users.

Shepherd and Yeo's appraisal framework attempts to redress this balance by making the 'needs of internal/external users' (2003, 157–61) a primary consideration and identifying information value as a key quality, but it does not provide an objective mechanism for measuring such value.

Shepherd and Yeo also rightly point out the importance of bringing together a range of views and opinions when it comes to making appraisal decisions, including representatives of the business unit, professional experts such as lawyers and accountants and, of course, the records manager and archivist. Where the effectiveness and practicality of this approach falls down, however, is by pointing to 'specialist committees' as the recognized way of bringing such a disparate range of views together. This would seem to risk re-imposing a very low ceiling on the scalability of such an approach and to dramatically limit the volume of records that any such committee could be expected to deal with. If Web 2.0 technology is likely to be a causal factor in increasing the volume of information to be appraised, why not seek to use it for our own purposes and to help automate and increase our capacity to deal with its consequences? This may enable us to pursue the collegiate approach encouraged by Shepherd and Yeo, but in a way which is equal to the task that confronts us.

The role of the user and demands placed on them

It is, of course, a fine line: we need the users, their expertise and their participation, but we must be realistic about the limits of their appetite and availability for contributing to our appraisal activity. It takes little time for the records manager to issue an edict that all records belonging to a certain series, or which are the result of a particular function, must be retained for a set period and then destroyed. It is a far more complex, demanding and labour-intensive process to actually ensure that this is carried out in a timely and controlled manner wherever such records exist. Moreover, it is a task that can rarely be accomplished by the records manager and his or her team alone; instead it requires the active involvement and participation of those who create, use or hold the records in question. We, as records managers, ignore this at our peril. Making the act of appraisal a process divorced from the routine use of information (as it so often is when conducted on an periodic basis as part of a 'black bag' day or clear desk drive) simply reinforces the impression in the minds of the user that this is some rather arcane concept, divorced from their own role and requiring attention for only a couple of days each year before slipping back into obscurity. When the task is conducted in this manner interest is likely to be minimal and the depth of analysis shallow, as people try to 'blitz' their office as quickly as possible before returning to their normal activity.

As the volume of information our organizations hold increases, so we must have a greater appreciation and consideration of what we expect from our users as part of the appraisal process. We have already seen that the attitude of many users to information management tasks in the Web 2.0 environment is varied and often, apparently, contradictory (i.e. their willingness to tag, but not to add metadata). As records managers, we must become far more knowledgeable about such factors and begin to appreciate aspects of workplace psychology so that we can understand how people view their working environment, their attitudes to the information they create and the tools at their disposal. By doing so we may well find ways of tapping into messages and patterns of behaviour that are attractive to our user base, while still achieving our own objectives.

Conclusion: one size does not fit all

The subject of appraisal is, and has always been, of central importance to the archive and records management professions and from what we have seen is likely to continue to be so into the Web 2.0 world. The question is, what form appraisal should take, what should its objectives be and how must we alter our methodologies and the tools we employ to achieve them.

Through these past two chapters I have done little more than scratch the surface of this vast topic. In particular, it is worth re-iterating the sentiments originally expressed in the Foreword, regarding this book's unashamed focus on the impact of Web 2.0 technologies on the management of records and information. Though these two chapters have, through necessity, touched on other areas, this concentration on what Web 2.0 may mean for the way we carry out appraisal has always been at its core and has accordingly influenced the arguments put forward. In many organizations, particularly those operating in tightly regulated industries, arguments about keeping everything and the importance of assessing the value of content for future reuse may seem of minor consequence, compared with the need to identify and preserve the evidence and the audit trail. Appraisal, like all elements of records management, must operate at multiple levels and within vastly different environments with fitness for purpose the only truly constant goal. It is the fitness for purpose of our existing appraisal methodologies for the Web 2.0 world that have been examined during these chapters and, to varying degrees, been found wanting, but this does not automatically imply that they are not still relevant when managing other types of record in other circumstances.

With this in mind, the time has come to turn our full attention to how we should seek to reinvent records management for the Web 2.0 world. We have explored the evidence for its arrival, discussed the nature and extent of its likely impact and raised concerns about how records management as we know it may struggle to cope. Now it is time for me to nail my colours to the mast and to try to define the direction records management will need to take and to flesh out exactly how it should be changed to face this challenge.

References

Report of the Committee on Departmental Records (Grigg report) (1954) Cmd 9163, HMSO.

Shepherd, E. and Yeo, G. (2003) *Managing Records: a handbook of principles and practice*, Facet Publishing.

PART 3

Records Management 2.0 and the future of records management

CHAPTER 11

The 10 defining principles of Records Management 2.0

Questions addressed in this chapter

- Are we really now in a position to be able to define what we mean by Records Management 2.0?
- What are the general principles that should define Records Management 2.0?

The difficulties of being specific at this point in time

Hopefully, the preceding chapters have helped shed light on how technology, through the rise of Web 2.0, has changed our world over the past few years and also demonstrated how many of the techniques and methodologies currently employed by records managers may cease to be relevant, or practical, in this changed world. What remains is to begin the process of defining how records management needs to change in order to meet these challenges; I suggest we call this Records Management 2.0.

In an ideal world, what would follow would be a step-by-step, practical guide to managing Web 2.0 based information according to records management principles, which could be picked up and adopted by any organization. Unfortunately this is not possible at this stage, not least because no-one, including myself, currently has all the answers. We are now operating outside the records management 'comfort zone' and merely finding new ways of saying the same thing, based on the same well worn concepts, is no longer applicable. I would be the first to admit that I don't even know all of the questions yet, let alone the answers, and it would be unwise and arrogant to pretend otherwise. What I have described in these pages has to be the start of a much bigger conversation and much longer journey. We must also be prepared to join with others as we travel and to engage with experts in web technologies, with other branches of information and knowledge management and, yes, with our users.

That does not, however, mean that the question of solutions and answers can be legitimately ducked altogether. The rest of this chapter and the one following present my initial thoughts and concepts: many may well prove impractical or unwise; some, while not in themselves achievable, may spawn related, more successful, future ideas; and maybe just one or two might find favour in their own right.

As we have seen throughout this book, technology is transforming our profession and the organizations within which we function at an unimaginable rate. This, of course, implies that changes round the corner in two, five or ten years time could sweep away what I have to say in these pages and make Records Management 2.0 equally redundant. This is an unavoidable risk and one of the curses, blessings or challenges (depending on your point of view) of living in our technocentric modern world. But the inevitable and yet unpredictable nature of technical change should not be taken as an invitation to wave the white flag and do nothing; it is, however, another reason to avoid being too detailed and too prescriptive at this early stage when the Web 2.0 landscape is still forming and emerging. Now is not the time for designing pre-formed, ultra-detailed methodologies but, instead, for thinking more in terms of adaptable, reuseable and extensible concepts.

The 10 principles of Records Management 2.0

With this in mind, what is perhaps required at this stage is a set of guiding principles. Such principles should help define what we mean by Records Management 2.0 and provide the framework within which more detailed thinking can occur and more concrete solutions be designed. Of course, over time it is quite conceivable that these principles may themselves need to be refined and replaced and this is to be encouraged; after all, if they cannot stand up to rigorous examination it is questionable whether they deserve to be considered as guiding principles at all.

It is worth stating that these principles are not intended to replace the objectives of records management as currently understood and articulated, but should be considered *in addition* to them where the need arises. In many respects, the 10 principles of Records Management 2.0 are designed to help ensure that the objectives of traditional records management can continue to be achieved within a Web 2.0 environment. For example, Part 1 of ISO15489 provides the following definition of the benefits of records to an organization, all of which are assumed to continue to apply to Records Management 2.0:

Records enable organisations to:

- conduct business in an orderly, efficient and accountable manner;
- deliver services in a consistent and equitable manner;
- support and document policy formation and managerial decision making;

- provide consistency, continuity and productivity in management and administration;
- facilitate the effective performance of activities throughout an organisation;
- provide continuity in the event of a disaster;
- meet legislative and regulatory requirements including archival, audit and oversight activities;
- provide protection and support in litigation including the management of risks associated with the existence of, or lack of, evidence of organisational activity;
- protect the interests of the organisation and the rights of employees, clients and present and future stakeholders;
- support and document current and future research and development activities, developments and achievements, as well as historical research;
- provide evidence of business, personal and cultural identity; and
- maintain corporate, personal or collective memory.

It is hard to disagree with the above list; records can and should contribute to all of the above and it is the role of records management to make sure that they do. Given the radical changes that Web 2.0 based technologies are on the cusp of bringing to our organizations and our culture I offer the following 10 principles required from Records Management 2.0 to ensure that the records, *and other internal information*, created within a Web 2.0 context continue to play the vital role all agree that they should.

Records Management 2.0 must be:

1 scalable to an (almost) infinite degree
2 comprehensive: with the potential to address all aspects of the management of information throughout its lifecycle
3 independent of specific hardware, software or physical location

4 extensible and able to absorb new priorities and responsibilities as they emerge

5 potentially applicable to *all* recorded information

6 proportionate, flexible and capable of being applied to varying levels of quality and detail as required by the information in question

7 a benefits-led experience for users, that offers them a positive incentive to participate

8 marketable to end users, decision makers and stakeholders

9 self-critical and positively willing to embrace challenge and change

10 acceptable to, and driven by, the records management community and its practitioners.

Reference

ISO 15489-1:2001 *Information and documentation – records management – part 1: general*, International Standards Organization.

CHAPTER 12

Expanding on the principles

Questions addressed in this chapter

- Do the concepts currently transforming resource discovery offer us the possibility of a new basis to our records management theory?
- Is it really conceivable that we could trust the collected wisdom of our users to play an active role in the appraisal process?
- Are we witnessing a psychological shift away from a generation of users who wish to keep everything private towards one who wants to share everything?
- Are there any constants in the Web 2.0 environment that may provide us with a common platform for developing management solutions?
- How can we make sure that records management remains fit for purpose in the future?
- How can we ensure that Records Management 2.0 is embraced both by records managers and the users on whom they rely?

For the remainder of this book I shall attempt to put some 'meat on the bones' as far as the 10 principles of Records Management 2.0 are concerned. However, it should be noted that what follows is *not* intended as a definitive description of what each principle means; instead they collectively represent just a few of my own thoughts as to the implications of each principle and what they may mean for the nature of records management, combined with some suggested theoretical ways forward. It is quite conceivable that there are many other possible interpretations of each principle; what follows is designed to provoke further thought and debate, not to be definitive.

Principle 1: Scalable to an (almost) infinite degree

The limiting factor when it comes to the scalability of records management is, largely, due to its reliance on the participation of records managers themselves. More specifically, it is the way in which records management has created systems and processes that place records managers at their heart and rely on them to establish the policies, update the standards or initiate the procedures. As we have seen, this is true whether we are talking about developing a file plan, maintaining a metadata schema or appraising records.

The IT community has discovered that there is another way, and that is to place a greater degree of trust in the users themselves. The concept of tagging information for resource discovery, based on user-defined folksonomies, is not only infinitely scalable, it actually gets more effective as more users participate. For example, if only three people have tagged a particular resource as featuring a tree while another two have tagged it as being a bush there may well be doubt as to which it actually is; but if 1400 users have tagged it as a tree and only seven as a bush the chances are that we can place our trust in the wisdom of the crowd. Of course, it is not foolproof, not least because not everyone's opinion is always equal: perhaps those seven who described it as a bush just happen to be seven of the world's leading horticulturalists who have perceptively identified a rare plant that deceives the casual observer.

Regardless of such limitations, it seems as though this democratization of resource description, despite its faults, is finding favour with a new generation of users. Perhaps the inevitable price to be paid for scalability is a partial trade off of quality in favour of quantity? I doubt that such a compromise will come easily to the records management community, but I fear that in the circumstances it may well prove a necessary, if bitter, pill to swallow.

The technology to allow users to tag their own information does, of course, already exist in countless guises. Most Web 2.0 applications include their own integrated tagging tools, whether it is for describing a blog post, an image in Flickr, or a video clip in YouTube. A smaller number of what could be described as 'umbrella' tagging services also exist, such as Del.icio.us,[1] which allow users to bookmark specific pages held in an infinite number of websites and then to use tags as a way of managing, linking and discovering these pages. But, at present, Del.icio.us works at a level above that required for our purposes. It may allow users to tag individual web pages, but does not extend this functionality to enable tagging of 'deep web' content, for example documents within a Google Docs account and presentations within Spresent.

Perhaps what we should be seeking to develop is a folksonomy service that can penetrate deep content, at an individual object level, across multiple service providers. In the absence of the client-server architecture that we currently rely upon, such a service would help provide the beginnings of the logical 'glue' organizations require to connect the records and information their users are beginning to hold in numerous services within the heterogeneous Web 2.0 world.

Relieving the records manager from the near-impossible task of creating and maintaining a metadata schema and file plan capable of handling hundreds of millions of items spread among countless systems certainly offers the promise of scalability. Furthermore, in doing so it potentially creates the space required for the records manager to carve out a new role. As has already been touched upon, the wisdom of the crowd is far from foolproof; could the skills and time of the records manager be better employed in the role of arbiter and quality controller? Certainly, within an organizational setting, it could be possible for the records manager to look at ways of improving the accuracy and effectiveness of 'their' crowd; for example, by linking a user's profile with their tags it should be possible to give certain people's views a prominence and weighting that reflects their expertise and position. That way, the authoritative voice of the expert horticulturalist may yet still be heard among the general chatter of the amateurs when it comes to defining which is a tree and which is a bush.

This is to envisage the records manager in a less hands-on and more strategic guise and is a theme which will recur as we explore the other principles. For if we take the records manager out of the front line when it comes to resource discovery perhaps this provides us with a blueprint for how we can achieve the required levels of scalability in all other aspects of records management practice.

In a sense, the web technologists who have brought us the concept of the folksonomy have done the hard work for us. They have succeeded in reversing the established logic that had previously underpinned resource discovery (i.e. that of structures, rules and standards designed by the few and applied to the many) and in breaking free from the assumption of centralized control – and what is more, they have proved that it works. We are now in the fortunate position of being able to take advantage of this new premise and to make use of it for our own ends.

To endlessly discuss the relative merits of whether tagging is any more, or less, accurate a form of resource discovery than a file plan, or metadata schema, is to miss the most important and interesting point of all. That is, that it is not really about resource discovery at all, this just happens to be one expression (indeed the only expression at the moment) of a much more significant concept: the possibility of using the wisdom of the crowd to manage the crowd. Once we accept this as an option it opens up a whole new world of possibilities allowing us to achieve the traditional objectives of records management but on a far larger and limitless scale.

Principle 2: Comprehensive, with the potential to address all aspects of the management of information throughout its lifecycle

We have already seen how the records manager is not, and cannot ever be, omniscient and that it is a potentially dangerous mistake for us ever to assume that we can be. The information creator is often likely to have a far more detailed and accurate picture of the significance of the function that created the information, its current and potential future value and its likely audience. This does not, of course, mean that the creators can assume the mantle of omniscience either. Their view may well be detailed and authoritative from their own particular part of the process or professional standpoint, but this alone is not enough. The accuracy and depth of their knowledge of the related functions and processes that rely upon the information they create may be similarly flawed, especially the further away from the act of creation the information travels. But what if we were able to aggregate this collected wisdom? What if we sought to capture the views not only of the information creator, but of all those who access it and make use of it from that point forth? Such an accumulation of knowledge about an item of information and its value would be far in excess of anything available to the records manager to date and may well now be possible, thanks to the very techniques and technologies that Web 2.0 is opening up.

Whenever critics of file plans start to question their use as the basis of resource discovery their defenders always (and quite rightly) point out that a good file plan should be the basis of much more than just resource discovery. It should also form the basis of a much broader suite of management tools and be used to define everything from security and access controls to retention management and the identification of vital records. So what if we were to take this same logic, but rather than try to use the centrally defined, un-scalable file plan, seek to apply it to the technique of user-defined tagging instead?

Let me explain what I mean. User reviews are an integral part of the Web 2.0 movement, whether it be reviews of books on Amazon,[2] films on LoveFilm[3] or consumer goods on any one of the endless number of online shopping sites. Such reviews by 'real people' are often a good guide – especially when accompanied by additional data indicating how many other people found that particular review of value (in effect a review of the review). Usually one only has to read through the first half dozen reviews to form a fairly accurate picture of the value or quality of the item in question which cuts through the spin and hyperbole of the advertiser's claims.

What if we sought to harness the views of the creator of the information and all its subsequent users in a similar way? This need not require the writing of a full 'review' each time a piece of information is created or used (something few users are likely to feel inclined to do) as there are other means by which an appreciation of the information's value at any point in time can be recorded. This may be in the form of a simple 'was this information of use to you?' type of question with a 'yes' or 'no' answer option, or perhaps providing the ability to rank an answer to the same question from a simple range of 1–5, dependent on its degree of 'usefulness'.

Nor would we necessarily be restricted to asking a single question. Of course, there is always a balance to be struck and we must always caution against over-burdening the user just for our own convenience, but it should, with further research, be possible to determine a limited number of questions we can encourage (but in the spirit of Web 2.0, never mandate) our users to address. Doing so would enable us, as records managers, to gain a much clearer impression of the true operational value of the information in question.

When it comes to appraisal, for example, it would be extremely useful to be able to ask everyone who comes into contact with a piece of information not only whether they found it useful, but also whether they feel it should be retained for, for example, another 12 months. Often, of course, there will be a clear link between information a user found useful and their view as to whether it should continue to be retained, but this will not always be the case. For example, a user may not have found an information source of use for the particular task they were attempting to complete, but can still appreciate its value for other functions and activities.

By asking the simple question 'Should we keep this for another 12 months', with a 'yes/no' response option, of everyone who accesses the information we will quickly start to build a picture of the *perceived* operational value of the information. Moreover, this is a question which would be equally valid when asked in relation to a written record, a multimedia resource or research data; it is also infinitely scalable and, as explained above, actually becomes more useful the more people who participate.

We must, however, acknowledge its limitations. It is certainly not foolproof and it is important to remember that the *perceived* value of information is not necessarily the same thing as its *actual* value. As any records manager will tell you, it is often the driest, most tedious record which is actually the most important when it comes to providing evidence and protecting the organization's legal interests. The identification and protection of such records is not best left to the user. Thus, what starts to emerge is a scenario whereby the opinions of the user base and the records manager start to work in harmony, each with an important and complementary role to play in the decision-making process. What Web 2.0 technology has provided us with is the means by which to collect and aggregate the views of the crowd and to present them as one collated and coherent view for the consideration of the records manager.

The appraisal process has always been a multifaceted one, usually assumed to require consideration of three main factors: operational need, regulatory/legal requirements and historical interest. By canvassing the opinion of its users we would be able to make significant strides towards a rigorous and scalable methodology for assessing operational need as the first phase of the appraisal process. The results of this initial sift can then be presented to the records manager for further analysis. How the view of the crowd is then interpreted and acted upon by the records manager will undoubtedly vary according to the nature of the organization and its appetite for risk. In some industries, a decision may be taken that if a certain percentage of users indicate that the information should no longer be retained, combined with a consistently low 'usefulness' score, the information in question can be automatically removed with no further analysis. In other situations, such a set of scores may simply act as the mechanism for flagging information considered to be a candidate for deletion, but still requiring further professional analysis to assess other possible legal or historical value before being cleared for destruction. Even in this latter scenario, where additional manual intervention is still required, the process will have made a significant difference to the scalability and reach of records management by short-listing the information requiring the attention of the records manager.

The aggregation of individual user opinions does much to even out their inevitable subjectivity. However, there are also other techniques by which we could further refine and add value to the opinions of users. Websites such as Amazon have long made use of their ability to track user behaviour on their site as a means of providing contextual information to other users, for example, through their 'Customers who bought this item also bought . . .' function. Such information could prove invaluable for the records manager who wishes to know the context within which a particular piece of information is viewed by users as part of the appraisal process. For example, if one seemingly trivial source is always used in conjunction with other records already known to be of high importance, this could well indicate a value which had hitherto escaped detection. Algorithms which are able to make this connection (i.e. repeated user interaction between a low-ranking and high-ranking piece of information) should be able to flag this as a warning if such an item is selected as a candidate for deletion.

Once the basic premise of capturing and making use of the user voice as an integral part of the management process is accepted, there appears to be no logical reason why it cannot be similarly applied across other existing areas of records management control, for example, when determining access controls. The majority of information stored in Web 2.0 systems and services tends to be openly and publicly available as a default anyway; after all, as we have seen in early chapters, the business model that underpins most such offerings depends on attracting a large number of users and a critical mass of content. For some content this might continue to be appropriate, even when used within an organizational context (for example multimedia resources), but this will not uniformly be the case – and certainly not for the kind of content that we would recognize as business records which may now be created within Google Docs and the like. Here, some level of access control is clearly required, as neither restricting all content to the creator nor making it freely available to all would be appropriate.

Without a central file plan to categorize such information or a central system able to extend its reach into a myriad of externally hosted web services, it is clear that a new approach will be required.

Until recently, any solution relying on the judgement of users to decide who could access their information is likely to have resulted in virtually everything being classified as private and restricted only to them. This is still a likely scenario with the current generation of users but may be less so in the future. One of the most striking trends emerging from the Web 2.0 generation is not only a willingness to share information but a positive desire to do so. Whether it be putting images of friends and family on Flickr, sharing your thoughts about life, death and politics on a blog, or just which web pages you most enjoy on Del.icio.us, there appears to be an overwhelming compulsion to tell the world. The detail of the psychology behind such changes is beyond the scope of this book, but its impact and its implications are relevant. Maybe, in five to ten years' time, we will be able to trust our users to view openness as the default setting (indeed, one suspects that the problem in the future may well be ensuring that users appreciate the sanctity of organizational boundaries – particularly given the increasing overlap between the use of information in their domestic and work lives, as discussed earlier).

So, when it comes to how we manage access control within the Web 2.0 world, perhaps again we must look at the role of the content creator and the broader crowd of which they are a part. Given the fundamental principle of openness that lies at the heart of Web 2.0, whether it be in terms of sharing your photographs, or allowing others to reuse and 'mash' your data, it would seem as though the default setting for any content created should be that it can be shared within the organization as a whole. Naturally, there will always be good reasons why certain information should have a more restricted circulation, for example, because it is confidential, sensitive, or contains personal data. In these situations the creator must be able to add a property to the item in question to declare that in their opinion this is so. This act of declaration should be the trigger to prevent general circulation of the information in question and to restrict access to a predefined chosen group. The Del.icio.us social bookmarking service currently operates on a similar basis, whereby by default all bookmarks added by a user are publicly viewable, but the facility to override this, and make a particular bookmark private at the touch of a button, does exist.

Of course, it is all very well to dream of a future utopia, where a new generation of content creators has the spirit of openness and sharing coursing through their veins and influencing their actions. In reality, there will always be some individuals who buck the trend and who, for whatever reason, are unwilling to share the work they do – even with their colleagues and peers. This is another example of a situation where the opinion of others can be used to moderate the views and actions of the individual. Perhaps, in this case, any request to restrict the circulation of information could need the ratification of either their line manager, or the records manager, before being confirmed, while also allowing anyone who comes into contact with the information (i.e. subsequent users) to influence its accessibility in the light of their own opinion. Once again, the general principle is of placing a greater onus on the judgement of the content creator, but within a constantly evolving, predefined framework, influenced by the broader user body and ultimately ratified by the records manager.

Principle 3: Independent of specific hardware, software or physical location

As we have seen throughout this book, the two main challenges presented by the management of information and records in the Web 2.0 world are volume and diversity. The shift towards user engagement and mechanisms for assessing the attitudes and behaviour of 'the crowd', as described above, has the potential to provide the level of scalability required, but currently lacking from established records management practice. On its own, however, it does not automatically address the problems posed by the creation and storage of content held on a range of disparate, unconnected Web 2.0 systems and services. The absence of a common technical architecture underpinning these services, in the way in which the client-server has underpinned our organizational infrastructure for the past decade or so, is clearly problematic. It appears to provide no tangible structure, no 'hooks' on which we can attach our solutions, and without it the concept of taking advantage of the crowd to manage the crowd – as outlined above – remains little more than an interesting theoretical proposition and a catchy sound bite.

Thankfully, it is possible to identify two elements that are always common, regardless of the number of services in question or who provides them. The first is the individual user and the second is the presence of the web. What we have witnessed throughout this book is the way we are currently seeing a transfer of the foci of ownership, management and control away from the organization and towards the individual user. As we have seen, this is evident through trends such as the use of the same systems, content and even user accounts for both domestic and work use and the 'straddling' of both these aspects of a person's life (when blogging for example). This may be an uncomfortable trend for many to accept, and will of course be felt at different speeds and in different ways from organization to organization and sector to sector. But rather than just discount it or worry about it we should see whether we can actually utilize it for our own advantage.

It may seem an obvious, even redundant, statement to make: to identify the web as universal presence within the Web 2.0 world, but, once again, it represents a potentially valuable tool in our armoury. To all intents and purposes the world wide web has replaced the client-server as the backbone of our information architectures, but of course it is not a perfect comparison. After all, the web is 'worldwide' and not, therefore, limited to the confines of any one organization. Yes, of course, it is possible to place artificial barriers around it and to contain it within a single organization in the form of an intranet, but this is not an easy solution to the problems we face for all the reasons alluded to throughout this book: the user preference for 'best of breed' external services; the declining barriers between our work and domestic lives; and the urge to contribute to, and take advantage of, the wisdom of the greater crowd.

So, what emerges is the need to build Records Management 2.0 solutions using web-based technologies, but with the individual user at the core. There would seem to be two main ways in which these twin constant factors can be most usefully combined for our purposes: at the application level, or as a Web 2.0 service itself.

The web browser is, of course, already an omnipresent interface between the individual user and *all* their web-based activity. Perhaps development of the browser itself for records management purposes could offer an interesting route forward, with the web browser becoming a single, consistent and controllable gateway to a range of otherwise unconnected services. Certainly, even those in the vanguard of the Web 2.0 movement who have purged their desktop of every other application are still reliant on the presence of a web browser as their gateway to the online world. In addition the development of open source browsers such as Firefox[4] and Epiphany[5] now provides both the canvas and a toolbox to enable unfettered research and development, but there, alas, the potential ends. The browser is far more wedded to the world of the desktop, than the web; for example, the browser that sits on my machine at work is not the same as the one which I use on my domestic PC – each is a completely separate 'physical' entity, even if I use both to access the same web services. As such, it lacks the quality of 'location independence' required to enable the user to manage the totality of their online information, regardless of the specific machine they happen to be using.

We must also acknowledge that the browser as an application is a pretty blunt instrument, unable to do little more than skim the surface of the web. While it is possible to capture individual resources held within some Web 2.0 services (for example to bookmark a particular image in Flickr) doing so is unsophisticated and far from scalable. Indeed, it is the limitations of bookmarking as a means of resource discovery that has led to the rise of social bookmarking services such as Del.icio.us. It is therefore difficult to imagine how the technology underpinning the concept of the browser could ever, alone, form the total answer to our requirements. It is unlikely to prove sophisticated enough to enable the user to define the range of properties relevant to a particular individual resource, plus because each instance of the browser is separate, and not by itself an integrated part of the crowd, it offers no means of aggregating the views and opinions of the user base, nor even of allowing the individual user to make use of the same tools regardless of which machine he or she happens to be using.

But just as the browser benefits from the presence of a service such as Del.icio.us as a 'plug in' to improve resource discovery and to bind the user to the wider web world, so, perhaps, this is the model that we should be seeking to expand upon for our own purposes.

For those unfamiliar with Del.icio.us, it may be worth summarizing its main functionality and the advantages it provides over the browser's own bookmarking facility. Del.icio.us is a web service which, once a (free) user account has been created, enables you to flag particular websites or resources that you wish to select for future reference. However, unlike with bookmarks or favourites within a browser, these selections are kept and are accessible from the Del.icio.us website and not just from the individual application you happened to be using at the time; this means they can be accessed regardless of the machine you are using or your location in the world. It is possible to download two 'shortcut' buttons onto the toolbar of the browser(s) you use most regularly, one of which enables you to access the links stored on your Del.icio.us account, while the second starts the process of selecting the page you are currently viewing as a new resource to be added to your Del.icio.us account. These two buttons help create a virtually seamless 'bridge' between the remote web service and the physical application being used at that moment as the user's main access route.

There are two other features which differentiate Del.icio.us from browser-based bookmarking. Firstly, users are free to describe each link they have selected by whatever criteria they wish, by ascribing as many free-text, uncontrolled tags as they like. This is a far cry from bookmarking or adding favourites, where only the title of the resource can be altered and where each bookmark must appear in one position within a hierarchical folder structure. Instead, the use of tagging creates graphical 'tag clouds,' where all used tags are displayed and each tag is given a font size and weight to reflect the number of times it has been used as a descriptor – thus providing, at a glance, a graphical representation of the most frequently used tags within that user account. The second, and most significant, difference is the connection between an individual user's account and the broader population of Del.icio.us account holders. For every time a user starts the process of selecting a new web page to tag, Del.icio.us will provide a number of popular tags which have already been employed by other Del.icio.us users when describing the same resource. Of course, the user is completely free to ignore these suggestions, but, in my experience, they are often accurate and useful (even if augmented with a few of my own) – evidence of the wisdom of the crowd in action. These links between the user and the crowd are also used to encourage additional resource discovery. For every page or resource that I tag, Del.icio.us tells me how many other account holders have tagged that resource and allows me to access their full list of selected pages. The logic is that as we both shared an interest in one resource, perhaps I would be interested in other pages they had linked to, but which I have yet to discover. Finally, it is worth pointing out that most Del.icio.us accounts also illustrate the trend towards use of services that span the totality of a user's life, with links to resources that are of interest to their work, their hobbies and their family life.

Take up of Del.icio.us and other social bookmarking services such as Digg,[6] reddit[7] and StumbleUpon[8] has been so successful that many popular websites will include the facility to add pages from their sites directly to a user's account. Site authors are clearly aware of the viral power of such sites to spread awareness and encourage use of their resources and are, therefore, keen to make it as easy as possible for this to occur.

So, maybe a Del.icio.us-style Web 2.0 service that plugs into the user's browser, provides the ability for them to access it anywhere and strikes a balance between the autonomy of the individual and the influence of the crowd, could form the basis of a Records Management 2.0 solution. It certainly appears to have merit, and to offer the promise of a hardware-, software- and location-independent platform that would allow users to assign properties to their Web 2.0 resources as they see fit, influenced by, and at the same time influencing, the opinions of the crowd. Even as currently designed, Del.icio.us already begins to provide something approaching the depth of penetration required, enabling the user to select and tag at the level of the individual blog posting, YouTube clip, Flickr image, wiki entry or Office 2.0 resource. There are undoubtedly still many technical obstacles to overcome – particularly with regard to accessing and managing content stored in password-controlled accounts – but this still appears to be a very promising model indeed, and one from which may emerge the functionality required from any Records Management 2.0 solution.

Principle 4: Extensible and able to absorb new priorities and responsibilities as they emerge

Who, just a few years ago, could have predicted the technical, social and cultural trends which are today shaping the way information is being created and used? Who knows what the future will hold? The simple truth is, of course, that nobody does, and while we should all have half an eye on the horizon, we should not kid ourselves that we can ever know exactly what the future will be. This being so, we must be careful not to paint ourselves into a corner, or to develop systems or approaches that impose fixed limitations on our actions.

Most of the content of this book is a response to what I perceive to be the most pressing challenges we currently face, namely the sheer volume of information now being created and the diversity of unconnected systems within which it is now stored. But who is to say that these will continue to represent the biggest challenges in five or ten years' time? Maybe managing vast quantities of information according to records management principles will have become routine in a few years' time, and similarly we will have cracked the issue of managing information spread across disparate systems. Who knows where the future challenges may lie and what the priorities will be? All we can do is ensure that Records Management 2.0 is flexible and extensible enough to absorb new directions and priorities – whatever they may be.

The proof of the pudding will, of course, be in the eating, but I would hope that the type of possible Records Management 2.0 solutions that I have been exploring in this chapter will prove equal to this requirement. After all, the underlying concept of capturing, aggregating and utilizing the knowledge contained by the user community to inform (but not necessarily decide) management requirements is one which could be further extended as required. It is not possible, nor indeed desirable, to try to predict either what questions we may need to ask in the decades to come, or what methods of aggregation and analysis may be needed to address future, unknown, requirements. Nor do we need to try to predict what new varieties of Web 2.0 system it must encompass, so long as we are as confident as we can be that what is developed is extensible enough to bring them into the fold as and when the situation demands.

Principle 5: Potentially applicable to *all* recorded information

As we have explored in previous chapters, in practical terms much of the previous rationale for making a distinction between *records* and *information* is steadily disappearing. Interestingly, this does not signal a dilution of the records management cause, quite the opposite: it reflects the fact that *all* the information created by an organization, regardless of its formal status, would now benefit from the level of control that records management has hitherto provided for the minority. No doubt purists will still want to distinguish the record from other information or data and to champion its unique properties and importance, but I would beg to differ. For all the reasons explored in previous chapters, it no longer seems appropriate to restrict our field of vision to the small percentage of information that has been our traditional domain, and, indeed, we risk doing a grave disservice to our organizations if we continue to do so.

Of course, this is not the same as suggesting that all information is of equal value, as clearly it is not. There will always be some information that is inherently more important, either simply because of its content, or because of its evidential value and the importance of the process that created it. What Records Management 2.0 does, however, is to acknowledge the fact that *all* information is at least worthy of initial inclusion and assessment, even if it subsequently proves to be of little or no real value; what it doesn't do is simply *assume* this to be the case from the outset. Just as in law we are all innocent until proven guilty, so information should be assumed to be of value until proven worthless.

The advantage of Records Management 2.0 lies in its limitless scalability and, therefore, in its ability to encompass *all* recorded information. It represents a means of casting the net of management and control far wider than has previously been possible, or even thought necessary, to enable this fundamental assessment of value to be carried out. Those brought up to believe that appraisal is a complex skill, to be practised only by trained professionals, may still question the robustness of the methodology underpinning Records Management 2.0 and have concerns over the apparent rashness of trusting the 'wisdom of the crowd,' but it should be remembered that what is proposed is not without its safeguards and, for the most part, the results returned will be used to inform, rather than replace, the role of records manager as the final arbiter. It should also not be forgotten that the alternative (i.e. the status quo) will continue to see the vast majority of information held by organizations subject to *no* managed appraisal process whatsoever. So, perhaps for the sceptics, Records Management 2.0 should, at the very least, be considered to be 'better than nothing'.

Principle 6: Proportionate, flexible and capable of being applied to varying levels of quality and detail as required by the information in question

A strong policy framework has long been an integral element of records management and this should inevitably continue to be the case with Records Management 2.0. Thus far, this description of one possible interpretation of Records Management 2.0 has focused on the technical, but of course it must represent a much broader church than that. Technical solutions, no matter how innovative, must still exist and operate within a comprehensive and cohesive policy framework in order to be effective and fit for purpose. This is especially so when addressing the challenges posed by the rise of

Web 2.0, given the fundamental changes it brings to the relationship between individual users and the organization they work for, combined with the loss of physical ownership by the organization of many of the systems and services it previously directly controlled.

One of the most striking effects of Web 2.0 has seemingly been the empowerment of the user at the expense of the organization. Understandably, many organizations and their management will feel threatened by this shift and will seek ways of guarding against it – a concern which will inevitably vary in degree according to the sector and the nature of the organization in question. Though local factors and individual personalities mean it is hard to generalize, it would seem likely that commercial companies working in new technologies, professional services and creative arts (publishing, software design, advertising and IT consultancy, for example) may be more willing to leverage the advantages of Web 2.0; while those organizations working in heavily regulated industries (pharmaceuticals, engineering, etc.) and those with large, well established, 'traditional' bureaucracies (government departments, local authorities, etc.) will be most resistant.

This means that clearly articulated policy statements, appropriate to the individual circumstances within each organization, will be of crucial importance. Records Management 2.0 does not need to be an 'all or nothing' endeavour; indeed, I would go so far as to say that it should never represent the 'all'. What I have proposed is a solution designed to address a set of challenges posed by the rise of new technologies and the changes it both drives and reflects which cannot (in my view) be met by current records management practice. This does not mean that any organization should abandon 'traditional' records management wholesale; where it works we leave it alone, it is only where it doesn't that we need intervene. In some organizations, perhaps even in entire sectors, it may be perfectly sensible to take this light (maybe even non-existent) touch for now and for the foreseeable future. In an earlier chapter I made the observation that I, for one, would not fancy being a passenger on a plane designed by Wikipedia and I would stand by that remark. There are many organizations that carry out complex, highly technical and tightly regulated processes which create and require information of equally robust and accurate quality. The presence of Web 2.0 may be so lightly felt in such surroundings as to be almost imperceptible, at least for now, but I believe it is inevitable that over time the pressure both from within and without will push even the most reluctant organization further down this path. In the private sector, much of this drive may well come courtesy of the organization's marketing and customer relations staff: those who are paid to understand and respond to the demands and wishes of their clients, who will come to expect products and services encompassing the philosophy and technology currently driving the Web 2.0 movement. But, for now, where Web 2.0's impact is light or even non-existent, logic dictates that the same should be true in terms of the rationale for Records Management 2.0: where it clearly isn't broken, there is no need to fix it.

Perhaps in this situation, a clear policy framework which amounts to something along the lines of 'the use of any unauthorized external services or systems to create, store or manage corporate information is strictly forbidden; breaches of this will result in disciplinary action' represents a sensible and proportionate response – at least for now. That said, I would still encourage any organization taking this stance to treat such a position as being constantly under review as, for all the cultural, economic and social as well as technical reasons outlined in this book, it may well prove to be unsustainable at some point in the future.

But for those organizations, perhaps the majority, who have a pragmatic or only partially formed view regarding their attitude towards the pros and cons of Web 2.0, such policies will continue to play an important role in defining their position and setting the boundaries. Inevitably, in this situation the policy framework will end up being more detailed, more complex and more fluid. It may prove necessary to specify individual Web 2.0 services which are either authorized or prohibited and perhaps even what type of content is acceptable within those which are allowed. Indeed, more 'shades of grey' may well be required other than simply whether systems are authorized or prohibited. Further categories may be required to reflect the fact that the use of some systems is 'actively supported' (perhaps user training and a helpdesk facility is available or steps have been taken to integrate some aspect of the system with other 'corporate' systems), while others are 'authorized but not supported' (where staff are permitted to use a system but do so at their own risk and without the assistance of the organization).

Given the rate of technical change and the speed with which new systems suddenly gain market dominance (and equally quickly lose favour), there are considerable challenges implicit in the requirement to maintain such a policy framework, not just in terms of keeping up to date with what your users are demanding and what your organization is willing to allow, but also in communicating such changes to your staff in a meaningful way and integrating them into working practices and management controls.

Thankfully, the specific approach to developing a Records Management 2.0 solution that I have been advocating in this chapter meets this need for a proportionate and flexible approach. A records management Web 2.0 service, based along social bookmarking lines, could be extended to those systems authorized by the organization and blocked from being applied to any systems whose use is not permitted, either within the organization, or for use in association with 'corporate' information. That said, my own view is that we should only bar particular services or systems as a last resort, for as the next section explores, there is considerable advantage in developing Records Management 2.0 solutions that our users positively *want* to use, rather than simply being compelled to – and this requires creating as inclusive, comprehensive and user-focused an approach as possible.

Principle 7: A benefits-led experience for users that offers them a positive incentive to participate

The UK records management community has become quite adept in recent years at using a 'big stick' approach to ram home their message. The introduction of a series of legislative drivers, including the Data Protection Act 1998 and the Freedom of Information Act 2000, has understandably placed compliance at the forefront of our arguments. Staff are often ordered to follow procedures and commanded to comply with policies even when (as is often the case) the measures we introduce for the good of the organization may actually inconvenience or otherwise have a negative effect on the working life of the individual. Naturally, such a brief summary is an over-simplification and all good records managers will do their utmost to listen to their user community and ensure the measures they introduce are as sympathetic as possible to individual requirements, but ultimately the needs of the many (in the shape of the organization as a whole) must take precedence over that of the individual.

There is a large element of good sense and logic about taking such a hard line. All organizations have a moral, as well as a legal, obligation to obey the laws and regulations that govern the environment in which they operate, the vast majority of which are mandatory and non-negotiable. By and large, by signing a contract of employment each member of staff agrees to abide by all the policies and procedures that govern the operation of the organization and, in doing so, agrees to help ensure that it meets its statutory obligations. As readers of this book will be only too aware, compliance with some legislation (such as the two Acts mentioned above) relies directly on the way in which information is created and managed, while there also exists a whole raft of other laws with either direct, or indirect, implications for recordkeeping. It is clearly not for each member of staff to pick and choose which laws they wish to observe, just as they can't when driving a car. Unfortunately, however, the consequences of breaking the Data Protection Act, for example, are often less immediately apparent and severe to the individual than driving the wrong way down a one way street, or failing to observe a red traffic light. As a result, our current levels of compulsion and enforcement, backed up by the threat of punitive measures for non-compliance seem a necessary, if regrettable, reality.

The problem comes when we start to rely too much on use of the 'big stick' and begin to see it as the only weapon in our armoury. It is an easy position to fall into – after all, if we can always rely on the 'you must because the law says so' approach, why bother with anything else – especially anything which indicates a level of compromise or individual free will. While undoubtedly correct, adopting such a tone can have unintended and unfortunate consequences. As the old saying goes, 'one volunteer is worth ten pressed men', the records management version of which might be 'one optional tag is worth ten mandatory keywords'. Making it compulsory to enter descriptive keywords does nothing to ensure the quality, accuracy or relevance of the terms selected, and the same is true across the records management spectrum – right up to the use of entire systems. We may make use of the new corporate Electronic Document and Records Management System (EDRMS) compulsory, we may even remove access to the old network drives they have replaced, but this does little, if anything, to win over the hearts and minds of the users who have it in their power to make the system either a success or failure. Users will soon find ways around the use of mandatory, but unpopular, systems and even where all escape routes have been blocked off, what level of thought is likely to be given as to how a file is named, or where it should be stored, when all sense of enthusiasm, autonomy and ownership has been squeezed out of them? Or, alternatively, they may well just decide to leave and move to a job where they don't have to use an EDRMS. In fact, a colleague told me recently that he himself had done this a couple of years ago as, in his words, using the EDRMS implemented by his employer was like asking a plasterer to use a hammer!

The vision of a Web 2.0 workplace outlined in Chapter 4 was one largely dictated by user choice. Where the officially sanctioned system was found wanting, people started to look elsewhere and find their own solutions to problems: in particular, looking to those systems or services that they already have a favourable experience of using outside work. If Records Management 2.0 is to be successful it has to be popular, and for two main reasons. Firstly, because if it is not we will be no further forward in terms of user engagement than we find ourselves today; and secondly (and far more importantly) because we will be missing out on the enthusiasm and desire to participate that characterizes the Web 2.0 resources we seek to manage, and which is essential if we are to be able to gather, and make use of, the wisdom of the crowd.

In order for Records Management 2.0 to fulfil its objectives it therefore needs to be not only accepted by the general user community, but enthusiastically adopted, owned and embraced by them. It has to be something that content creators and users actively *want* to contribute to, for all the same reasons that they volunteer to review books on Amazon, comment on a YouTube clip, or share their bookmarks via Del.icio.us. As such, it must tap into the two ever present, but apparently contradictory, drivers currently fuelling the spread of Web 2.0: personalization and individual empowerment on the one hand, and altruism and mass-collaboration on the other. If ever we retreat down the familiar road of compulsion and enforced participation, the game is lost.

Adopting the functionality, format and style of Web 2.0 services that have already proved popular with users should hopefully go some way to ensuring that the kinds of approach to Records Management 2.0 proposed in this chapter receive a fair hearing, but it is not, alone, enough to guarantee the level of support required.

That can only be achieved by creating something that not only meets the needs of records managers and the organizations they serve but becomes adopted by, and even loved by, users as a tool which they (literally) can't manage without.

This may sound a tall order for a records management product, but could well be achievable if it offers answers to some of the problems that users face. Interestingly, I suspect that many of these problems are exactly the same as we have already identified as being issues at an organizational level, namely:

- how to manage the ever increasing volumes of information being created by individuals in their domestic and 'non-work' lives
- how to ascribe value to this information in order to make sensible decisions as to what deserves continued retention and/or storage on particular media (for example portable devices)
- how to manage consistently the information created and stored within various disparate online services
- how to draw together the information created and required as a result of the various disparate threads of their life (domestic, work, voluntary, clubs and societies, hobbies, professional interests, etc.).

If we were to develop and give away (and I do mean 'give away' in the sense of 'give freely, without charge') a Web 2.0 based records management service that people can use to manage their non-work information, and were then to introduce the exact same system into their workplace, we stand to reap the benefits of system-familiarity that we discussed in earlier chapters as part of the general appeal of leading Web 2.0 services. Even more so if we not only allow use of the same technology, but also the same user accounts, so that it does truly become the user's default tool for the management of *all* their online content. Who knows, perhaps such a service could reach the level of popularity currently enjoyed by Del.icio.us (after all, who a

few years ago would have predicted that classifying resources –
previously considered the specialist domain of the librarian – would
ever be so popular?). Perhaps then we could see a records
management-based YouManage service reaching the kind of level of
popular awareness and participation currently enjoyed by YouTube.

Principle 8: Marketable to end users, decision makers and stakeholders

Clearly the question of marketability is closely related to the previous
principle; after all, unless Records Management 2.0 meets the needs
of its respective user communities and stakeholders it will be
difficult, if not impossible, to market. Again, it is possible to see
where the records management profession as a whole may have
taken its eye off this particular ball in recent years, with selling
pitches which appealed strongly to certain groups (compliance
officers, lawyers, risk-averse senior managers) but which may have
left other groups (IT staff, content creators, mobile/flexible workers,
'new media' developers, risk-tolerant senior management, etc.)
rather cold. Any Records Management 2.0 solutions need to take
this on board and ensure that they meet the needs of all their
stakeholders and potential users, rather than becoming over-reliant
on one particular group and one particular message.

This undoubtedly requires the records management profession to
pay far more detailed attention to how the people we wish to use our
systems actually think, behave and work than has hitherto been the
case. It has long been a source of puzzlement to me that a profession
that relies so heavily on the actions of others to achieve its objectives
seems to pay so little attention to understanding those on whom it
relies. This is a big potential topic and a detailed examination of it
lies beyond the scope of this book. Here it suffices to point out that
in a world where technology provides the user with a greater degree

of choice, power and control than ever before it is absolutely vital that we understand what motivates information creators and users and, wherever possible, seek to build our approaches around them. Naturally, this statement is fraught with dangers and difficulties – after all the user is a notoriously fickle beast and there is no guarantee that what attracts them today will be the same in a year's time, but nonetheless, this is the challenge that confronts us if we are to succeed in attracting people to use whatever it is we have to offer.

We may well need to find ways of including disciplines such as psychology and organizational behaviour in our professional canon, not just by issuing the odd survey, but by commissioning and utilizing rigorous, professional, academic research. Such work may help us understand what truly motivates users and why: for example, why they seem to react so differently when carrying out two such seemingly similar tasks as adding user-defined tags or centrally defined metadata. Once we understand such subtle but important nuances we are in a better position to incorporate this learning in our system and process design.

Another angle altogether when it comes to marketing is the possibility of an organization making use of existing Web 2.0 services and bringing them into the organizational fold by applying their own veneer of branding and functionality over the top of the generic product. You can already see this trend at work in the way organizations have taken the Google search engine and embedded it within their own websites, either as the search engine for the site, or as an access point to the wider web (or both). Another interesting example I came across recently is with the online DVD rental service, lovefilm.com. As an existing user of the service I was interested to see the *Guardian* newspaper[9] offering what sounded like a very similar service. Indeed, upon closer examination, I understood why it sounded so similar: the *Guardian* service is actually the very same LoveFilm service offering the same products, at the same terms and conditions, but with a style and branding of its own.

Perhaps this offers the promise of another path to achieving Records Management 2.0. As we have seen, there are some integrated suites of Web/Office 2.0 products beginning to emerge, for example those provided by Google and Zoho.[10] A realistic compromise solution for some larger organizations may be to work with these providers and to create their own contextual layer which sits over the top of a 'ring-fenced' set of approved externally hosted services. This would offer their staff access to *some* Web 2.0 services and *some* of the advantages they provide (remote access, for example), but would also offer the organization the opportunity not only to brand these services in their own corporate colours, but potentially to develop additional management tools to be used by their staff when accessing their particular instance of the services in question. Of course, the problem with compromises is that they risk pleasing nobody: users might not wish to be restricted to using only those few, corporately branded services, out of the myriad available, and management might feel that outsourcing the storage and management of their corporate information in this way exposes them to an unacceptable degree of risk without offering enough in return. Either way, it is a further example of how marketing will undoubtedly play a vital role in the success, or otherwise, of Records Management 2.0, while also serving as a reminder that we should be willing to consider radical new approaches to help meet the challenges of a changing world.

Principle 9: Self-critical and positively willing to embrace challenge and change

I think I can safely predict that many readers of this book will have disagreed with some, perhaps even all, of what I have said within its pages. This is inevitable whenever you challenge the status quo and dare to stick your head above the parapet; and as one of the main aims of this book was to stimulate further debate and move the agenda forward I actively welcome dissenting voices of all shades and strengths. At least, I do so provided such counter-views stem from a considered, logical disagreement with what I am proposing and are not simply a knee-jerk reaction to my daring to challenge existing orthodoxy.

The archive and records management professions are innately conservative; indeed we rightly pride ourselves on taking the long view, a position that is entirely appropriate when you consider that we are responsible for record collections often spanning several centuries. But as we have repeatedly seen throughout this book, while our professional objectives should remain absolutely fixed and solid, our methodology and working practice need not do likewise. The two are not inextricably linked and indeed it is not just desirable but necessary that we are prepared to fundamentally challenge the way we do things, to ensure that we are able as a profession to continue striving to achieve our objectives. Today's heart surgeons can trace their values and objectives back to ancient Greece and the time of Hippocrates but, thankfully for us, the techniques they employ to achieve them change virtually out of all recognition every few years. We now have to be prepared not only to accept but to embrace a similar rate and degree of change, if we are to retain any semblance of professional relevance in the years ahead.

A prerequisite of such continual professional reinvention is the need to constantly challenge what we do and why we do it. There should be no sacred cows. Every practice must be open to rigorous examination to assess its continued fitness for purpose, relevance and impact. When practices pass such examination we can have added confidence in what we do; but when they fail there should be no hesitation in finding alternative approaches to meet the new challenge, or help to improve quality.

Such constant critical self-examination must be an essential ingredient of Records Management 2.0. Rather than continuing to plough our furrow regardless of the maelstrom of change swirling around us, we need to respond to it as quickly as possible. Many of the techniques that underpin records management have served us well for half a century, but everything has a finite shelf-life. Whatever form Records Management 2.0 takes, it will inevitably have the same finite usefulness; we should not shy away from this but actively embrace it. After all, the organizations in which we work and the technology which drives them are subject to similar constant reinvention.

Constant self-examination will hopefully make our profession and its practices more robust, relevant and effective. But while this introspection is essential, it is not, by itself, enough. Nothing is better for challenging your beliefs than having to explain them to others and this must be an important aspect of this 9th principle of Records Management 2.0. Of course, it is essential to our profession that we have our own societies, such as the Records Management Society,[11] our own conferences and our own professional literature. But, we must also look further afield and engage with the other stakeholder groups that will be critical to the success of Records Management 2.0: namely users and the web development community. It is essential that we talk to others, pay heed to what they tell us and be prepared to rethink our approach if it fails to convince. Records Management 2.0 will only succeed if it becomes a broad-church movement where we actively embrace discussion with a range of voices and make a concerted effort to seek out those who to disagree with us to find out why, which of us is wrong, and, if we are wrong, what we can do about it. We should be willing to apply our own professional belief in the value of appraisal to our own methodologies, as well as to the information we manage. We must adopt a rigorous approach to determining whether the way we currently do something still has value, and if it doesn't we must be prepared to accept this and to remove it from our professional canon. Such a continual process of renewal should be embraced as a positive and cathartic movement, enabling our profession to remain fresh, invigorated and capable of meeting the challenges it will continue to face.

Principle 10: Acceptable to, and driven by, the records management community and its practitioners

But all of this talk about broad-church movements and the need to engage with wider audiences will count for little if Records Management 2.0, in whatever guises it takes, is not accepted by, adopted by, and driven by the records management community. Of course this doesn't mean that the issues I have been addressing through these pages must suddenly become the paramount priority for all records management practitioners. As we have seen, in many industries the impact of Web 2.0 and Office 2.0 may not be felt for some years to come and in the meantime there remains the same range of operational and strategic issues to address, few if any of which may require the type of innovations I have been describing. And even in those organizations that are already beginning to feel the impact of Web 2.0 this does not mean that we should drop everything else, tear up the rule book and set off in a radical new direction. Our response must be proportionate and for many at the moment this may mean little more than maintaining a watching brief on this agenda. However this must not be taken as an invitation to bury our heads in the sand. When you see a storm gathering on the horizon you may not need to take cover straight away, but only a fool would choose to leave their coat and umbrella behind and set off for a stroll regardless.

We must never lose sight of the fact that it is not illegal to impersonate a records manager. We are not invested with some divine or legally appointed right to manage information that is denied to all others. If, for whatever reason, we fail to do this effectively that is not the end of the story – others will soon fill the void, and, indeed, they already do.[12] They may not be records managers and they may not approach it as we would wish, but approach it they will, leaving us in the cold and perhaps failing to deliver the kind of robust, sound and comprehensive solution that we are capable of and that our organizations require.

Though others, undoubtedly, have a part to play, I remain convinced that records managers have a huge and vital role in moving this agenda forward. We possess a combination of skills, values and concerns that are unique to us and are the product of a long and distinguished process of professional development stretching back more than half a century. The choice of the term Records Management 2.0 as the umbrella heading to encapsulate the various principles and approaches I have been suggesting is a deliberate one; for no matter how radical a departure from orthodox records management much of this may seem, I remain convinced that a solution firmly based on records management principles is what is required and that my interpretation of Records Management 2.0 has the potential to deliver.

Whatever form Records Management 2.0 takes, it is essential that it is palatable to records managers. If it remains something of only tangential interest and novelty value to the profession it is hard to see how we can help fashion a response to the challenges we face that is consistent with our professional ethos and acceptable to our requirements. Records Management 2.0 should not be viewed as a replacement of established records management theory, merely an extension and addition to it. If this book helps persuade even a small proportion of the profession to acknowledge the challenges that lie ahead, to consider how best we may address them and to be prepared to use their skill and experience to advance this cause, it will have been worthwhile.

But of course the end of this book marks only the start of the journey. With luck it is a journey that will be continued through numerous conference papers, journal articles, blog postings and discussions over a pint in the years ahead. I, for one, find it stimulating to be working in a field where no one knows the answers, where the rules of the game are being constantly rewritten and where each of us has a genuine opportunity to make a difference to such an important and emerging area. With luck a little of this enthusiasm will have filtered through to the pages of this book and I only hope you have enjoyed reading it as much as I have writing it.

Notes

1 http://del.icio.us/ [accessed 3 March 2008].
2 www.amazon.co.uk [accessed 21 February 2008].
3 www.lovefilm.co.uk [accessed 21 February 2008].
4 www.mozilla-europe.org/en/products/firefox/ [accessed 22 February 2008].
5 www.gnome.org/projects/epiphany/ [accessed 22 February 2008].
6 www.digg.com/ [accessed 22 February 2008].
7 http://reddit.com/ [accessed 22 February 2008].
8 www.stumbleupon.com/ [accessed 22 February 2008].
9 www.sofacinema.co.uk/visitor/home.html [accessed 4 March 2008].
10 www.zoho.com/ [accessed 28 February 2008].
11 www.rms-gb.org.uk/ [accessed 28 February 2008].
12 For example: courses in information rights being run by university law departments; books on retention schedules being produced by the Institute of Chartered Secretaries and Administrators; the development of institutional repositories within universities by learning technologists and library staff; and the

majority of work being conducted on digital preservation by IT staff, archaeologists, librarians and others, but rarely archivists or records managers.

Index